LIMBO

BY CAROBETH LAIRD

Encounter with an Angry God
The Chemehuevis
Limbo
*Mirror and Pattern: George Laird's World
  of Chemehuevi Mythology* (in preparation)
Pilgrim and Stranger (in preparation)

LIMBO

Carobeth Laird

CHANDLER & SHARP PUBLISHERS, INC.

Novato, California

For obvious reasons, the name of the nursing home, Golden Mesa Nursing and Convalescent Home, and some names of individuals are fictitious.

Library of Congress Cataloging in Publication Data

Laird, Carobeth, 1895—
    Limbo.

    1.   Nursing home patients—Arizona—Biography.   2.   Laird, Carobeth, 1895—
I.   Title.
RA997.5.A7L34   362.6'11'60926   [B]   79-10937
ISBN 0-88316-536-8 pbk.

SIXTH PRINTING, 1994

COMPOSITION BY MARIN TYPESETTERS

For the Michelsons,
who saved my life

CONTENTS

ACKNOWLEDGMENTS

The period of my life with which this volume deals was one of great stress and uncertainty. Before I proceed to acknowledge the contributions of the persons who have assisted directly in the preparation of *Limbo*, it is only just to offer some measure of gratitude to those who helped me to survive this difficult time and to write about it afterwards.

Harry Lawton (Chairman of the Editorial Board, Malki Museum Press), as always helpful and supportive, read *Limbo* in manuscript and reassured me as to its literary quality.

Micki Michelson and her family made a place for me in their home in Poway, California, where I am loved and cherished. Here I wrote *Limbo* and here I am continuing to write.

Mary Mitchell, Wayne Culp, Pamela Munro, and Mabel Axtel were among those who visited me in Indian Hospital. Although when she saw me I could not articulate distinctly, Pamela gave me confidence that I would recover and go on working. Mabel's daily visits brightened my existence.

My very special thanks are due Anne Buffington-Jennings. She has neglected her own work to forward mine, and she gave me encouragement when I was filled with self-doubt. Anne did the preliminary editing of *Limbo* and put me in touch with Jonathan Sharp of Chandler & Sharp Publishers.

Jon Sharp has been considerate and supportive, and his editing was meticulous. Charlene Sharp offered valuable constructive criticism based upon her expertise in nursing.

My granddaughter, Cheryl Weller, retyped the first draft of the manuscript, thereby saving me many hours of labor.

Clara Dean expertly prepared the draft that was offered for publication.

Ralph Michelson furnished the author's photograph.

I thank Gordon Molson for his unflagging guardianship of my interests; and Helen Brann for her enthusiastic efforts on my behalf.

These acknowledgments would not be complete without a word of gratitude to the physicians, surgeons, and nursing personnel who have helped to prolong my life. Now I shall see *Limbo* in print—and perhaps other books now in preparation.

C. L.

LIMBO

PROLOGUE

If you expect a tale of horror, of filth and overt cruelty, read no further. This does not purport to be a sensational exposé of nursing-home conditions. It is instead an account of one person's efforts to hold onto sanity and identity in an atmosphere which was, by its very nature, dehumanizing. It dwells of necessity upon those trivialities of daily routine which loom so large in the lives of the helpless and isolated.

That I was at this time as isolated as I was may seem incomprehensible to those who know I have seven living children. Without going into detail which would serve no purpose here, I can only say that either long-standing estrangement from my children or their own then-present personal difficulties made it impossible for me to appeal to any of them for a home.

Recently a friend sent me a newspaper clipping telling of a senile patient in a Southern California nursing home who was found drowned in a therapy pool, still strapped in her wheelchair. Such an event would have been impossible at Golden Mesa; it had no therapy pool.

One also hears of facilities where elderly patients lie untended in their own filth. The management of Golden Mesa prided itself on the fact that patients in that institution were kept up and active. True, old people sitting for hours on end in wheelchairs, frequently fastened in for their own protection, sometimes had what were euphemistically referred to as "accidents." Once in the dining room a square-jawed old lady who reminded me of two dominating and dignified women I have known at different periods in my life, began to scream that she had to return to her room. She was told to hush, to control herself, to eat her dinner. She had to come out openly with the cause of her distress, informing the whole room that she had wet her diaper and that the urine burned intolerably, before an indignant aide would wheel her out. And ambulatory old gentlemen sometimes went about in wet pants.

However, I continue to believe that Golden Mesa was, at least during my residence, a superior institution within its price range. The quality of food served the patients was what one might expect to find in a poorly run prison, and the underpaid and overworked (and frequently ill-trained) aides were sometimes impatient and to a certain extent neglectful. But incidents of cruelty that I witnessed were few and petty.

If I seem to dwell with obsessive repetition upon the functions of the body in this work, you must remember that the lives of those in Golden Mesa, and similar facilities, essentially revolve around eating and excreting.

I am sorry to say that I have recently heard indirectly that conditions at Golden Mesa are now "worse than ever." I know that Ann Keim left shortly after I did. More recently other older workers, including Dorothy Williams and the cook, have been let go. They were "too old," and possibly it was necessary to pay them higher wages than less experienced young workers would accept.

I can only hope that eventually the United States of America will find a way to deal with its aged in a manner befitting its wealth and claim to civilization.

PART I

Shadow in the Desert

1

I awoke rather suddenly. The night was very dark, very still, its silence broken only by the reassuring hum of the air conditioner. There was no rumble of thunder, no lightning split the sky. No coyotes yelped in the hills, no wild burros bumped and snuffled around the house or violated the night with sudden brays. After a few moments I turned on the light and looked at my watch. It was exactly three o'clock. I had been born precisely seventy-nine years and twenty-four hours before in a lonely house surrounded by the hot dark of a July night in Texas. I remembered that my mother had said, "They wrapped you up and laid you on the bed beside me. Then Mrs. O'Hare and the doctor went back to town and left me alone with you." The Mexican servant girl had run away hours before. She had taken fright at the screams accompanying a long and painful delivery. Of course my father was there, but apparently he didn't count. . . .

After two or three attempts I got up, took firm hold of my walker, and made my way to the bathroom with extreme caution. I was alone except for my sixteen-year-old grandson, asleep at the far end of the sixty-four-foot mobile home. Wayne was a sound sleeper, no amount of hollering was likely to wake him. If I fell, I would be in for several hours of extreme discomfort. But I got to bed safely, took a tranquilizer, and put out the light. I wanted to go back to sleep quickly, not to spend the hours till daylight dwelling upon a precarious and uncertain situation.

The mobile home belonged to my daughter Georgia, who was at that time Secretary-Treasurer of the Chemehuevi Indian Tribe. She had left the previous Wednesday (this was Sunday morning) to attend to some tribal business in Independence, several hundred miles away, intending to return Thursday morning. But climbing up the Panamint Gorge from Death Valley a wheel had come off her station wagon. She now lay injured in a hospital in Lone Pine, how seriously we had no way of knowing. The girl who would have been more or less available to look after Wayne and me had finally broken with her Indian boyfriend and left for her parents' home. Tearful but resolved, she had baked me a birthday cake, packed up, and taken her departure from Chemehuevi Reservation and the Colorado River country. A good move for Connie, and one I was glad she had taken. But it left me in a quandry. Unfortunately, I couldn't care for myself, and I had literally nowhere else to go. I was deeply concerned about Georgia, but—as I think must always be the case with the old and helpless—there was a very real concern for myself.

This was not the first time in my life I had reached what appeared to be a dead end. Always, perhaps at the last moment, a way opened. The thing was to keep calm, to pray after my fashion (not altogether Christian, but frequently expressed in the Christian idiom), and to wait it out. I lay in the soothing dark, confidently awaiting the drowsiness that precedes sleep.

Instead of sleep, pain. Sudden, violent pain around the heart, quite unlike anything I had ever experienced in that region. My reaction was, to say the least, odd. All I could think of was Red Foxx in television's *Sanford and Son*, putting his hand over his chest and exclaiming, "This is the big one! Elizabeth, I'm coming to join you!" I lay there giggling, exclaiming silently, "This is the big one!" How unexpected!

How ironical! I'd never in my life had heart trouble; and recently my one prayer had been, "Don't let me die in the desert." Now the room was filled with a presence, unmistakable, darker than the night. Almost every night for two precarious, painful years I had prayed, "Into thy hands I commit my spirit"; now I could only laugh to myself and think—when I thought at all—about a television comedy. Then the pain was in the pit of the stomach. Still around the heart but extending itself to the pit of the stomach. It was as if I had swallowed a large hot rock. I thought, remotely, about ulcers. Then, still holding on in heart and stomach, it jumped down into the lower right of the abdomen. A doctor in Escondido had said, "You have a diseased gallbladder. You have a large gallstone, but it doesn't seem to be troubling you." He hadn't suggested removal.

Now there was a great deal of pain. I didn't writhe and I don't remember hearing myself groan. I felt it, but with a certain detachment. I was at the same time experiencing and observing. There must have been at least partial loss of consciousness. Wayne says I called him, sometime after daylight, I presume. I don't remember talking with him. He says he was frightened. He went first to the Indian neighbors, the Antones, who also happened to be the nearest neighbors. They didn't know what to do. They told him to go to the Mitchells.

It was broad daylight—midmorning, or anyway that is what it felt like. Mary Mitchell was there, and Peggy Berger, a retired practical nurse who lived down at Havasu Landing, on the California side of Lake Havasu. I was quite collected. I asked Mary to take me to Indian Hospital at Parker (Arizona), where, as the widow of an Indian, living on a Reservation, I would receive free medical care. They weren't equipped to do much of anything there—even cast broken limbs—so serious cases were flown to the large Indian Hospital in Phoenix. I knew and liked Dr. Bertman, head of the hospital in Parker. He would surely give me something to relieve

the pain and send me to Phoenix. Which seemed pretty pointless in the face of the dark angel, but the game had to be
played out.

Mary asked about bedroom slippers. I didn't have any.
I told her I had to use the beat-up black shoes beside the bed
because they had a lift on the right heel. A robe? Only the
pink quilted one, and it was far too heavy. I suggested a short
peignoir. It didn't come quite to the knees and didn't close
down the front. But it seems it wouldn't be proper to take
me in just my nightgown. So in some way the two women—
neither of them young or vigorous—got me into the wheelchair, and down the steps, and into the back seat of Mary's
car, which had a quilt spread on it. I was wearing a long thin
well-worn pale green nightgown, and the peignoir, and the
beat-up shoes. It seems peculiar now, but we took no other
clothing for me, no purse, no glasses, no walker, no identifi-
cation of any kind. But this was an extreme emergency and
there didn't seem to be any point in taking things. I don't
think any of us believed I would be coming back.

The heat was like a club. The sky was partially overcast,
giving an illusive appearance of coolness, and rainstorms were
visible towards the mountains. We had had two or three days
of hard, intermittent rains with flash floods, and the road to
Havasu Landing was a horror. Bad enough when dry, the
deep gullies were now real hazards. We came off the dirt road
and on to the pavement and the going got better, but at Havasu Landing Mary said, "We'll never make it to Parker." She
feared that Chemehuevi wash and perhaps other big washes
would be raging torrents.

"All right," I said, "take me home and I'll 'tough it out.' "
(This was the time of Watergate, and a certain phraseology
came naturally to mind.)

Peggy said, "This woman has to have medical attention."
She was as abrupt as Mary was gentle, and I couldn't overrule
her. Actually, I wasn't trying to overrule anyone. My body
was in its own private cocoon of pain, my mind passive,
detached.

Deputy Dennis came by. It was his job to patrol all the Reservation side of the Colorado River, but fortunately, just now, he was down at Havasu Landing. Mary and Peggy explained the situation. He said he was sure something could be done. A boat had tied up there for refueling. Soon four men carried me aboard and deposited me on a narrow bench. It was a private pleasure boat, but for a long time afterwards I thought it belonged to the Coast Guard, and wondered dimly that a Coast Guard ship should have chintz-upholstered seats. Lake Havasu was choppy, the sky had darkened again, and the wind was up. The ship-to-shore radio crackled constantly. I don't know if they radioed for the ambulance or if Deputy Dennis had phoned. I was in no hurry to cross the three miles of water. In that remote, detached state of mind I knew the boat ride was something I would have enjoyed in that existence now fading.

Then we were tied up at the landing in Lake Havasu City, Arizona, and men from the ambulance were helping to carry me. I had wanted to visit Lake Havasu City. We could see its lights sparkling from our front porch. It was a synthetic enclave of modernity in the limitless desert; a good place to shop, people said—expensive, but not any worse than Needles. But it was eighty-four miles by road, and few people on or near the Reservation had boats. (The Mitchells had one, but it was undergoing repairs; and Peggy had a small one, unsuitable for transporting a sick person.)

The trip by ambulance to Lake Havasu Community Hospital was short. The driver didn't turn on his siren. I heard him reporting that "the patient's condition seems stable at present." I was mildly, remotely amused. I remembered a previous trip from Poway to Escondido when the siren had screamed all the way, although my condition had been far less desperate. Perhaps, I thought, that had been a new driver, anxious to try it out. (The pain intensified. Part of my mind was silently screaming for relief. And another part, quite calmly, took note of the weather conditions, people, glimpses of buildings.) .

Mary and Peggy had not crossed the lake with me. At the hospital I was on my own. I gave my name and address, and explained that I was not a local resident, and that when I said my post office was Havasu Lake, California, I did *not* mean Lake Havasu City, Arizona. I answered questions about insurance. I had Medicare and Blue Cross. No, I did not have my cards with me but I could remember my Medicare number. I gave my age, and said my medical records were either at Indian Hospital, Parker, Arizona, or Palomar Memorial Hospital, Escondido, California. I gave the telephone number of Georgia's hospital in Lone Pine and of Margaret's home in Del Mar. (Margaret is my youngest daughter.) I signed a paper, or papers.

Then I was in a room with another patient, a Mexican woman my age or a little younger, and there was a hypodermic. The pain dulled, and everything got very, very fuzzy. Somewhere in that period there was an X-ray. Then things cleared up, and a doctor, very kind, very frank, said that I had to have immediate gallbladder surgery, but at my age and in my physical condition, the chances of coming through it were not good.

I said, "OK, go ahead."

(The doctor who was to perform surgery, Dr. Hardtke— that's the spelling, I think—a humane person and a skillful surgeon, telephoned both Georgia and Margaret before he operated. He told them frankly that I was "sinking fast" and could not last through the night without surgical intervention and at best my survival was doubtful; afterwards he called again to tell them that I had come through much better than anyone could have anticipated.)

People came to move me. I must have voiced some objection, for I have the impression that something was said about my condition distressing the other patient. Probably they merely said that they were going to prepare me. Perhaps I was groaning or making a disturbance. I only remember being very quiet in my mind, very peaceful. And it seemed to be towards evening—a gathering dusk, although of course the hospital lights must have been as bright as usual. I do not remember any formulated thoughts, which indicates a unique condition; my stream of consciousness always flows to the accompaniment of words. In fact, I find it hard to conceive of unverbalized awareness.

2

I came to consciousness gently, in a room with a nurse standing by me. The room was dim, but the dark presence was as if it had never been. I wasn't particularly surprised when the doctor said, "You don't have a gallbladder anymore." There were a lot of things I didn't have, including physical sensation. When I did speak, my voice was slurred and strange, and it was a long time before I could articulate distinctly.

There soon seemed to be a good bit of activity, all concerned with my body. I think I already had an intravenous (IV) going in my left arm. Now they were working on my right arm, doing a "cut down," reminding me of that time remembered as in a dream when my sixth child had been stillborn. When the IV was in place, a nurse inserted a catheter to drain urine. I had always shuddered at the prospect of anyone undergoing this procedure, imagining it to be very painful. But because the nurse was skillful, or my senses were still numb—or perhaps because my notion had been a misconception—there was very little sensation and none after it was in place. Then a tube was inserted in my throat and I was told to swallow and keep swallowing until it went down into the stomach. This wasn't pleasant.

I had always slept with my feet crossed. Now I was told I mustn't, it was bad for the circulation. So there I lay, spread-eagled, not quite sure that a successful operation was worth it, yet not really very uncomfortable. After an indeterminate time, I was thirsty. "No, positively nothing to drink," a nurse said. Then another nurse said I could suck on some ice chips. This afforded my very first sensation of pleasure.

I suppose the place where I awoke is called an intensive-care unit. There was a nurse on duty at all times, in fact I had the impression of two or three people at the desk opposite my bed.

The room contained three beds, possibly four, separated by curtains. The lighting was subdued. I don't remember any routine that separated day from night. But I have the distinct impression that it was morning when a woman's voice from beyond the curtain said, *"Tengo hambre."* Apparently no one in the room understood Spanish, because with great effort and in very broken English, the voice demanded a hamburger. As nearly as I could make out, broth was offered and emphatically rejected. "No! *Quiero un* hamburger." The nurses were repeating incredulously, "She says she wants a *hamburger.*" They were amused, and more than a little shocked.

The voice belonged to the woman who had been my roommate briefly when I was first admitted. I learned later that she had had some sort of an intestinal obstruction and had been brought in with an immensely swollen belly and in great pain. As soon as the obstruction was removed and the anesthesia wore off she became fully alert, and saw no reason why she should not resume her normal eating habits. She did not stay very long in intensive care.

It must have been the next day that I complained to the doctor that the tube was making my throat sore and asked when it would be removed. By that time Dr. Hardtke had left for some sort of a convention, and Dr. Stoker, whose patient I was supposed to be, had also had to leave for a few days. I think it was Dr. Harvey who replied clearly, if inelegantly, "As soon as you fart."

I said, "No problem. Just let me get up and sit on a commode, and there'll be no difficulty." At least this is what I intended to say. My speech, like everything else, was uncoordinated. After a period of discussion, the catheter was clamped
shut and I was eased out of bed, onto a commode. I don't
know how this was accomplished, with IVs still in place, but
it was done. Now I sat facing the head of my bed, and saw
that I was connected to an instrument that measured heart
action. The little green light bobbed across the screen, and
again I thought, "Just like in television." However, I wasn't
sitting there to observe. By what must have been a direct action of the will I achieved the desired expulsion of gas, and
the next time the doctor came by, the tube came out. Not
long afterwards (the next morning, perhaps?) he ordered,
"Pull all catheters." I have the impression that a nurse was
tempted to demur. But of course she didn't.

The next step was broth, brought in on a tray and served
with a flourish. I don't wonder my companion in misery had
rejected it. The color and flavor were as appetizing as if
a chicken had walked through clear, hot water. I had a clear
vision of that chicken doing his duty in the kitchen.

Then I didn't need intensive care anymore and I was going
back to my room. Strangely, I didn't want to go. It was like
being expelled from the safety of the womb. As long as I was
in a precarious condition, I didn't have to think of the future.
Now I was helpless as a newborn infant, with no one to care
for me, nowhere to go. A brief time in the hospital—and beyond that, what? The body, with its relentless unreasoning
instinct for survival, was at cross-purposes with a mind that
could see absolutely no future.

I was back in the room with the woman who had demanded a hamburger. She may not have been getting hamburger, but she was having toast and eggs for breakfast, and
coffee, and I think even a little strip of bacon. I still had hot-
water-called-broth, with the addition of jello and tea. But it
wasn't because of food that I envied her. It was family. Her

husband came, a gentle dark-faced old man in a wide-brimmed felt hat that made me think of George; and various grown daughters, all solicitous of Mama, friendly with each other, all willing and able to cooperate in caring for their mother. I thought, if George hadn't been so much older than I, if he were still living, if our children were united instead of at sword's point. . . . If you could step back into the past and adjust it just a little, this could be my family coming to visit, and soon I would be going home with a husband who, after all these years, was like a part of me; home to a little farm with married daughters living not too far away and taking turns helping till I got on my feet.

Only George had been dead thirty-four years, and the children were scattered, and there was no little farm to go back to. Worst of all, I hadn't really been "on my feet" in a long time, and now the prospects seemed slight of my ever attaining that state. With short and careful steps, staying close to the wall, my roommate walked to the bathroom. The nurse said, "You ought to walk a little." I said, "I can't without a walker." But when the walker was brought, I couldn't even stand holding onto it. There was no coordination and no balance. The shock of the operation had deprived me of what use of my legs I had previously had, small enough after a twenty-year siege of arthritis and peripheral neuritis.

The room was light and pleasant, rather large for a hospital room. I could see across the street to what appeared to be a public building—I think they said it was a post office, and I thought to myself that that was probably all I would ever see of Lake Havasu City, and that not distinctly, because my distant vision was poor without glasses. This blurring and softening of faces probably fed that fantasy that my roommate's family might have been my own. A nurse discovered that I had a little Spanish and asked me to translate something. My roommate's face lit up, she launched into a flood of delighted speech. "*Señora*," I implored, "*Hágame me el favor de hablar mas despacito.*" But there was no damming the flood. I could only smile and try to look pleasant. After a day or two, husband and daughters took Mama home, and I had the room to myself.

Georgia had got someone to drive her home. This was very risky, yet probably for the best, for in the hospital at Lone Pine there had been no proper diagnosis of her injuries and she still had no idea how serious they were. Peg Berger and Mary Mitchell brought her across the lake in Peg's boat. It was a rough trip and she fainted on the way over. When she came into my room, she was obviously ill, and seemed to lapse into unconsciousness once or twice as we were talking. Mary and Peg took her to Dr. Harvey's office for X-rays, and I understand that the whole experience and the return trip were very bad. She was in no condition to take care of herself, let alone a virtually helpless mother. This was for her the beginning of a long series of stays in various hospitals, interspersed with other accidents and illnesses.

I was soon moved to another room. My new roommate was WASP, retired, living alone, very anxious to return to her own home. Our intercourse was pleasant, though not intimate. Through her and her visitors I glimpsed what must have constituted a rather large segment of Lake Havasu City society; moderately well-to-do retirees, happy to be living in Arizona, enduring the summer's heat for the sake of year-round sunshine. They were one and all politically conservative, active principally in pursuit of the good life.

My new roommate was concerned with the extent of damage her property might have sustained in the recent flood. I now learned that the rains which had flooded washes on the California side had wreaked havoc on Lake Havasu City. This "planned community" had been built without reference to the natural contours of the land. The fragile desert pavement had been bulldozed away, washes had been filled in and homes built on top of them. The elaborate drainage system that nature had perfected through thousands of years was ruthlessly destroyed. Houses had been built and landscaping planted on beautiful level lots. Much of this had been swept away in the flash floods that occurred shortly before my birthday. Now I learned that for two days before my admission the hospital had been without lights and water, except for a feeble emergency power system and water for drinking. Now no trace remained of this chaotic condition, although a nurse remarked that she still had to wear hip boots to get from her doorway to her car. Visitors assured my roommate that her place had suffered minimal damage, and none at all to the house itself. For at least one woman, however, the picture was not wholly black; she was getting a complete redecorating job out of the insurance company.

Interest in the catastrophe was fast yielding to preoccupation with normal pursuits. Pool parties were the really big thing. This or that woman had drunk too much and made a complete fool of herself, and so-and-so was not going to invite her again. Scandal vied with new recipes. There was gossip about bridge parties and probably also about golf, although this I don't remember. I gathered that golf was possibly not as big in Lake Havasu City as I later learned it was in Phoenix. Or perhaps my roommate's set had other interests.

All the rooms were equipped with color television. Since I still did not have my glasses, I couldn't watch with any satisfaction, but I turned up my sound when the news came on. Impeachment proceedings were coming to a climax. I didn't discuss politics with my roommate. I assumed, perhaps erroneously, that she was a diehard Nixon supporter.

Dr. Harvey was also my roommate's doctor. One morning he began to pull the drainage tubes from my incision (at first it felt as if he was pulling out an intestine) and did the same for my roommate. She had had, I believe, an operation for deep abscesses somewhere in the kidney region. She was ambulatory, eager to go home, but Dr. Harvey said she must wait till all drainage had ceased.

I was also ambulatory, in theory. The only trouble was that I couldn't walk. Sometimes with the aid of the walker I accomplished four or five steps between my bed and a chair, sometimes as many as six on the way to the bathroom. Then in an instant all coordination was gone. Or I might get over to the chair and after sitting for half an hour or eating a meal (I was now on a soft, fat-free diet) be unable even to stand when it was time to get back to bed.

Yet if it hadn't been for the sense of pressure brought about by the fact that Medicare would only pay for a limited time after surgery, I might have drifted into an almost euphoric state. So many times at intervals during the preceding two years I had said to myself, if I could only be clean and safe, I wouldn't ask for anything more. Both nurses and nurses' aides were incredibly kind, kinder than the attendants in any hospital in which I have been before or since. Since I did not like to use a bedpan, I was lifted up day or night and helped to pivot onto a commode (or more accurately, a chair that was used to give showers) and taken to the bathroom. There was a little Canadian aide who was often on night duty. When she maneuvered my embarrassingly dead-weight body onto the commode in the small hours of the morning and when I tried to thank her, in speech almost as uncoordinated as my legs, she answered cheerfully, "It's what I'm here for, luv," or "You're really not *that* heavy, luv." Somehow it was my impression that even the stereotyped endearments with which nurses address patients (especially the old and helpless) in all hospitals and nursing homes had here a ring of authenticity. The aides varied widely in education and training—there was, I remembered particularly, a large blond woman in a bright red dress (which I suppose meant she wasn't really a full-fledged aide) who used fantastically bad grammar and had a weird theory to the effect that the reason I couldn't walk was because I wasn't plumping my walker down on all four legs at the same time. But all were uniformly kind and willing to respond.

It also seemed to me that the doctors served with extraordinary devotion. I know there were nights when Dr. Harvey didn't go off duty.

Victor Kunkel, a business acquaintance of Georgia's, came to see me soon after I came out of intensive care. And after that his wife, Janie, came every day. She was a small, pretty, dark-haired woman, intensely but not oppressively religious, a member of some fundamentalist church (Church of God, I think), bringing up her five boys by a previous marriage to practice Christian virtues. Through my contact with her I came to have a respect for religious views which I had hitherto tended to scorn as primitive. "By their fruits ye shall know them." In her case the fruits were not a hell-and-damnation proselyting but a serene and uniform kindness. It was a practical kindness, a love for mankind freely expressed, that contrasted strikingly with the brittle and superficial attitudes of many of the retirees.

Best of all gifts, Janie brought me books—gift books and loan books. My eyes were focusing well enough to read, though not without difficulty. (Fortunately, I am not farsighted and did not need my glasses for reading.)

So now I was clean, safe, cared for, and reasonably comfortable. Outside the sun beat down in merciless strength, and sometimes the hot wind blew, but the air conditioners functioned quietly and efficiently. Sometimes at night lightning ripped across the sky, but there were no more disastrous storms. The serpent in Eden, the worm gnawing away at my cocoon, was my imminent expulsion in all my helplessness into a world which had no place for me.

Dr. Stoker was back from vacation and back on my case. He was young, competent, delighted with my progress. He said I really wouldn't need the sort of care I was getting in the hospital much longer. I asked if the hospital needed my bed. He said, No, they weren't at all overcrowded; but Medicare would only pay for two weeks after surgery. I called Elizabeth, my oldest daughter, in San Diego. She said she could let me have enough money for three or four more days, if the rates weren't too high. I had enough in the Needles bank (if I could get hold of my checkbook) for possibly three days more. But I had the dreadful feeling that in a week's time I wasn't going to be walking. Actually it had been a long time since I had walked well enough to be out on

my own. The social worker came with files and documents.
She asked searching questions and gave me papers to sign.
I said to Dr. Stoker, "I suppose you'll have to set me out on
the hospital steps." He said, "Don't worry, we won't do that.
We'll work something out." He spoke vaguely, not too hope-
fully, of a nursing home.

It was then that I thought again of Indian Hospital at
Parker. Dr. Stoker telephoned Dr. Bertman. Yes, they would
take me in. The Public Health Service would even pay for my
further stay at Lake Havasu Community Hospital if I wasn't
well enough to move. To my great disappointment, Dr. Stoker
said I was perfectly able to leave.

I learned that my gallbladder, removed hastily and with
little hope that the patient would survive, had been gangrenous and terribly enlarged. But the surgery undertaken under
such desperate circumstances had proved eminently successful, and I had made—as I have a habit of doing—a phenomenal
recovery. The only trouble now was that I was unable to care
for myself and without means to pay for any kind of assistance, let alone the sort of care that would eventually enable
me to function as a productive individual.

But for the moment the problem was solved. For years
I had endeavored to discipline myself not to look beyond the
immediate need and its immediate supply. And that had been
hard, for I am a congenital worrier. Now, as my mental faculties gradually emerged from dormancy, this discipline paid
off. I was able to anticipate my stay in the Indian Hospital
with interest. It would, to say the least, be an experience.

Now on a certain day—the fifth of August, I think, but it
might have been a little later—the nurses' aides tied up in
a plastic bag the books and the crocheted doily that Janie
had given me, and put the planter Elizabeth and Margaret had
sent me in a cardboard carton. Elizabeth told me that when
she ordered flowers to be wired to me, she had tried to specify
violets. But the florist thought the idea of violets in Lake
Havasu City in late July was hysterical. So she told them to
do the best they could and I had received a small planter with

two or three hearty succulents and cut yellow daisies—which soon withered—stuck here and there. Violets and maidenhair fern were my favorites. There had been violets growing against a shady wall in the yard of the house in Escondido I bought after George died. And long ago, before we were married, when I was at my parent's house in San Diego, we had taken a walk down into Mission Valley; and climbing back, up a steep, chamiza-covered hillside, we had come across a miniature ravine, not more than a foot deep, with maidenhair fern growing along its sides. I had wanted to dig up a clump to take to my mother, but we had nothing with which to dig. Mother had not approved of my walking with George, and would have been only slightly placated by the gift. George had been born in the desert, had lived in the desert until we met, when he was forty-eight years old. Now, even though the shadow had lifted for a time, would I still die in the desert? George had been dead these many years. Him I would not see again. Would I see maidenhair fern and violets, or even roses (fresh, not plastic), which I also loved? Now I was going back to Parker, where George and I had met. What fate waited for me there—and afterwards?

The ambulance sent by the Public Health Service was, characteristically, an hour or two late. No matter, I didn't have to pay for it. (Though I didn't at the time realize it, I hadn't yet paid for the ambulance with the screaming siren that had taken me from Poway to Escondido the previous May.)

The driver and his assistant were white men. They were not interested in me or I in them, though I would have thought their curiosity might have been piqued by the fact that they were hauling a white woman to Indian Hospital. The nurses and other personnel back at the hospital had shown friendly concern. I had said good-bye to those who were on duty when I left, knowing that I would miss them as persons, not merely for the scrupulous care they had given me. But I had been too fuzzy to get names and addresses. Besides, I had no scrap of paper to write addresses on, no purse in which to store anything. Except for the books, the doily, and the planter, I went out as I had come, with nothing but the pale green nightgown, the flimsy, too-short peignoir, and the beat-up black shoes.

Although it couldn't have taken more than an hour or so, the drive seemed a long one. As I had when I crossed the river, or again, as I lay in intensive care, I wanted time to stand still. Again, there was that clinging to the present, that reluctance to face an uncertain future. I pulled back the curtain an inch or two and through this slit watched with myopic vision the desert terrain. We made only one stop, at a gas station. When the motor went off, the air conditioning of course went with it, and immediately there was that tremendous assault of heat. The word "heatstroke" has always seemed to me peculiarly fitting.

Then we were pulling up to the ramp at Indian Hospital. There was the bright lawn; the sprinklers gave their illusion of coolness, and the pink and white oleanders, old and thriving, seemed more like brightly flowering trees than shrubs.

3

There were eight beds in the women's ward. I think that all of them were filled except the one to which I was carried. Although the faces of my new neighbors were blurred, I had the impression of seven pairs of dark, guarded, faintly inimical eyes. They did not disturb me. I felt nothing but friendship for these women.

My bed was by an outside window at the end of the well-lighted room farthest removed from the bathroom and air conditioner. The latter was old, and functional only by fits and starts. It didn't do any good to look out into the blinding sunlight and remind myself that it must be considerably cooler inside. The hot stagnant air closed around me. I found myself gasping for breath, wondering if I could possibly adapt to this, thinking that death by heat prostration and slow suffocation would not be pleasant. For the first time I almost wished I had not so hastily reversed the prayer that had risen so spontaneously to my lips the previous April. . . .

I had been in Poway, staying with my friends, the Misbeeks, while Georgia completed the move from Los Angeles to Chemehuevi Valley. Marjorie and Ernie had given up to me their own bedroom and the adjoining bath. Marjorie and Micki

Michelson had driven to Los Angeles and brought me and as
many of my possessions as could be jammed into a small for-
eign station wagon borrowed for the occasion. Later Marjorie
and Ernie had gone back and brought my color television and
a few other treasures. I had my typewriter, also the cases of
Xeroxed copies of Chemehuevi myths I had recorded half
a century before. Marjorie put the typewriter on her sewing
table by the bed, and the first month I was there I did a little
work and completed a paper for *The Journal of California
Anthropology*. But just working myself into the chair in front
of the typewriter posed a problem in logistics. Pain in hip,
knees, and shoulders was as constant as breathing. To walk
precariously along the hall to the living room and occasionally
out to the car when Marge took me for a drive was the extent
of my activity. And sometimes Ernie or Marge took me in the
wheelchair just to reach the car.

One afternoon I sat in my wheelchair on the asphalt in
front of the garage, wearing a sweater and with something
over my knees and a scarf for my head. It had been an unusu-
ally cold and wet spring for Poway, but on that day, although
the breeze was cool, the sunshine felt delicious. This was a few
days after April 13th, the anniversary of George's death.
(What a scorching April that had been!) I sat there in the sun
and the breeze, with Ernie's lovingly tended flowers blooming
on either side of me, quiet and remembering what no one
else remembered. The fields, hills, and some late-leafing
trees were bright green. On the mountains brush and scrub
oak grew dark and vigorous. Up there the Vallecitos grade,
now wide and paved and not in the least resembling the steep,
rough, one-way dirt road that George had worked on, was part
of the road winding up towards Ramona. A faint blue haze
reminded me of the color of wild lilacs, now blooming there
as they had bloomed that blazing spring day so long ago when
my love had lain helpless by the roadside after the accident
that would indirectly cause his death. The memory was so
poignant, so real, so immediate that my whole soul was drawn
out of the present, suspended in timelessness. . . . I heard my-

self murmuring, "Lord, now lettest thou thy servant depart in peace." The sound of my voice shocked me out of my trancelike state. I thought, that is a death wish! I am not praying for death, I do not dread life that much, I want to die at the right time and not before. Lord, thy will be done!

Perhaps I didn't retract quickly enough. My unconscious had received some sort of directive. That night I did not sleep at all. My bed was littered with books, and after awhile I turned on my light and read snatches in this one and that one, and finally one called *Varieties of Mystic Experience*. Then I put out the light and thought rebelliously, even if I could attain release from the wheel of life, or absorption into the infinite, or whatever, I don't want it; when I die, if there's such a thing as life after death or reincarnation, I want to be with George. It seemed to me then that I could hear him whispering urgently in the dark, answering me, "Hon, it's been so long—this waiting's gettin' awful old." This long forgotten idiom rising suddenly from its burial in my unconscious had the impact of audible speech, although there was actually no auditory illusion.

I didn't sleep that night, the next, or the next. Then began the violent, wrenching vomiting till Marjorie could no longer care for me in her home and I went in the screaming ambulance to Palomar Memorial Hospital. There the attack was diagnosed as a bad reaction to medication I had been taking for arthritis, but obviously it was a gallbladder attack and I don't know why the doctors didn't insist on removing the diseased organ then and there. (Two years and much surgery later, I'm inclined to think that when they saw the need for other complex internal repairs which their tests must have revealed, they considered my age and decided not to intervene.)

Eventually the vomiting stopped, and the nausea, although it didn't stop, was manageable, and I went back, frailer and more uncertain than ever, to Marjorie's house. And on the tenth of May Georgia came and took me to Chemehuevi Valley—to seventeen straight days when the thermometer never fell below 110° in the daytime, to dust storms and occasional glorious thunderstorms, to fear and uncertainty and eventually to the presence of the dark angel, summoning me to death in the desert, not in the green and pleasant place of happy memories.

Lying there stifling in the Parker Indian Hospital, I thought, to what purpose? And wondered how long this tortuous and nightmarish journey would continue. It was in Parker that I had met George, fifty-five years and two months before. I had been a twenty-four-year-old student of ethnology, with good legs, strong enough to walk away from any situation. Life came full circle, but with what a difference!

Whether it was these thoughts, or the heat, or delayed shock from the operation, or a combination of all three, I really couldn't say; but that night I briefly lost contact with reality. I dreamed, and what the content of the dream was I don't remember, except it was a Paul Revere-type dream, a dream of terrible urgency in which it was necessary for me to get out of bed and warn someone of something. The lives of everyone there, perhaps the fate of the world, depended on it. The dream carried over into waking, and I screamed and kept on screaming, and demanding that I be let out of the hospital bed to do what I must do. I had no doubt that if only the bars were down I could walk, run, fly to do what had to be done! The lights were on, people were standing around my bed telling me to be quiet, to be ashamed of myself, I was disturbing the other patients; and a nurse, a white woman, was slapping me briskly first on one cheek and then the other. She gave up and bustled away, and unaccountably I turned to the Indian girl sitting watching me with folded arms, and an expression of mingled disgust and contempt on her face. "I know you are compassionate, I know you will help me! Just let me get out of bed! Everything depends on it!" She replied only with a look of—if possible—intensified disgust.

I must have been making quite a bit of noise. The nurse came back, and other people, all horrified at my conduct. Something called a "restraint" was put on me, a sort of big, heavy gray bra with heavy straps tied in the back. But it wasn't tied to anything, and I don't know why it was needed, for I hadn't strength enough to sit up unaided, let alone to provide a threat to anyone or to myself. Then my bed was hastily rolled out and down the hall, to a small room with no one else in it.

Suddenly I was fully awake. "Why are you putting me in here?" I asked.

"You were disturbing the patients. The other ladies need their sleep."

"I'm sorry. I couldn't seem to wake up from a bad dream. . . . Can't you take this off? It's hot."

A kinder voice said soothingly,"Just keep it on till morning."

After a bit I fell asleep—I don't know whether or not I had had a sedative. This little room was blessedly cooler than the ward.

In the morning a nurse came in, said, "What's this thing for?" and took off the restraint.

I was grateful, and doubly grateful for a room to myself. There nothing was said of moving me back to the ward.

There was no outside window in this room, and looking through an open doorway across the hall I saw, in the room opposite me, what to my nearsighted eyes appeared to be vertical bars. I must have been still not quite rational. I jumped to the conclusion that this was a place of confinement for potentially dangerous patients. Several days later, coming back in a wheelchair from talking over the phone to a granddaughter who had heard of my plight and called me from Kingsville, Texas, it became clear even to my faulty eyes and overactive imagination that the bars were on a high crib in the children's ward; but not before I had told Mary that I *believed* I was confined to a part of the hospital with barred windows, and Mary had responded amiably, "My grandmother, the nut." It was cheering to speak with her, although she was in no position to help me.

How long did I stay in the private room? A week? Ten days? Perhaps even two weeks? It was a comparatively pleasant time. Dr. Bertman continued the mild sedative before meals to control nausea that had plagued me in Lake Havasu

Community Hospital and put me on an unrestricted diet. "If there's anything you can't handle, you'll soon find out," he said. There was much I didn't even attempt to eat. The food was hearty and ample, adapted to the needs of people accustomed to eating quantities of whatever they could get. Desserts looked appetizing, but cakes and puddings were made of the same heavy, gluten-rich flour that was distributed to indigent Indians, and were tough and heavy. But once there was a raisin bread pudding made of white bakery bread, and I ate almost the whole serving. Often there was a whole, peeled hardboiled egg on my breakfast tray. The nurses' aide who brought it always asked, "Are you sure you don't want this?" and popped it into her mouth.

I saw much more of the nurses here than I would later see as a patient in the ward. They and the aides were uniformly friendly. The one who had sat in scorn by my bed the night I had the nightmare did not, to my relief, appear. Some of the nurses were congenial—particularly a Mrs. Skallit, a strikingly attractive woman who had trained in some large Jewish hospital and had also worked in a nursing home.

The cook noticed how little food on my tray was eaten. One afternoon, entirely of his own accord, he came to me and said, "I'm having beans and fry bread tonight, and I know that'll be too heavy for you. What would you like?" We settled on canned pears and cottage cheese. After that he consulted me almost daily, and served me a modified diet. When I thought I couldn't handle fried chicken, he said it would be no trouble at all to make me a little chicken soup. The cook wore a voluminous white apron, usually soiled, and a chef's cap. I never asked his name or his tribe, but I know that he was kind to me. His face is one of the few from this period that is distinct in memory.

Except for the chronic hip trouble, the arthritic shoulders, and a curious tendency to sudden losses of coordination (for which no reason, medical or otherwise, has ever been found), and old age, for which no cure exists, the healing process was swift and inexorable. One morning Dr. Bertman led a small procession through my room. Tagging behind him were the two other full-fledged doctors on his staff, and the young student doctor (his name I remember, because it was Dr. Livingstone), and bringing up the rear a young woman with long blond hair, also, I presume, a medical student. Dr. Bertman pulled my sheet back and my nightgown up, and his entourage gathered round. He indicated the paling scar that marked my incision. "Will you look at that? This woman was operated on for gangrenous gallbladder only four weeks ago. Did you ever see a skin like that? And you must remember that this woman is seventy-nine years old." Exhibition concluded, the group moved on, accompanying the head doctor on his rounds through the minuscule and ill-equipped hospital.

On Sundays a parade of another sort straggled through, by ones or twos or threes. These were the representatives of numerous small fundamentalist churches engaged in soul-saving activities on the Reservation. I was learning tolerance and courtesy. Once I would have snubbed them cruelly; now I talked with them, received their pamphlets (I had nothing else to read, no access to the books packed away in the cardboard carton), and said, Yes, I would be glad of their prayers, prayer never harmed anyone.

I had one other visitor, Mabel Axtell, a Bureau of Indian Affairs employee who signed vouchers for Chemehuevi Reservation expenditures for Georgia, and whom Georgia had often mentioned. Because she was Georgia's friend, working with her on the Bureau of Indian Affairs side of the fence, she had at first thought, from some obscure political reason incomprehensible to me, that it would be impolitic to visit Georgia's mother in the hospital. But to the lasting joy of both of us, kindness overcame prudence and she came to see me. Our friendship sprang into being fully formed. Mabel came every afternoon thereafter, with only two or three exceptions. This was one of those shafts of light in darkness that made existence tolerable.

In the private room I led a comparatively pampered existence. Once or twice a day a commode was brought in and I was helped over to it, and encouraged to try the walker. One memorable morning I walked clear around the end of the bed, but the next day two or three steps were the limit. The nurses and even the nurses' aides did not complain about helping me. When I slid down in bed, which because of the inertia of my body I was continually doing, I was pulled back up cheerfully. Once with a husky girl on each side I was pulled up so vigorously that we had a great laugh about my almost going through the wall into the men's ward.

The children's ward across the hall held one patient. She was petted, played with, coaxed to eat, treated with loving care from morning till evening. She had the run of the hospital, except that an effort, not always successful, was made to keep her (and all visiting children) out of the maternity ward. Sometimes she came in shyly and visited with me. I couldn't find out what was the matter with her except that she had been dangerously run-down, and now was nearly ready to go home. Her parents hadn't been to see her, not even once, I was told. I believe they lived up in the vicinity of Peach Springs.

I settled into an endurable routine. Then one morning a nurse said cheerfully, "You're going back to the ward today." "I like it here," I protested. "You're getting well," was the determinedly cheery response. "You don't need special care anymore."

This time I had the bed next to the bathroom, at the coolest end of the room. The occupant of the bed on my right was Elizabeth Welsh, a pleasant old lady considerably my junior. Welsh was as old a Mohave name as Laird was Chemehuevi, both dating back to the time when intermarriage with whites began. But Elizabeth apparently bore me no ill will, either for being white or for having been the wife of a Chemehuevi. She had a cast on her leg. When it was first broken she was flown to the big Indian Hospital in Phoenix to have it set, and when the time came she would be flown back to have the cast removed. In addition to the broken leg, she was diabetic, as were many of the other patients. It is a common affliction among Indian people. (I supposed most of them were also anemic. The standard treatment was intravenous, and at least three-fourths of the patients, all of whom were ambulatory, maneuvered themselves about attached to the old-fasioned IV equipment, which included a forearm strapped to a board.)

I had been free from the IV contraption for some time now and Elizabeth was also free of it. She was quite strong, and after her morning sponge bath sat happily in her wheelchair. We greeted each other and sometimes conversed a little. I usually initiated the conversations; but on one of the rare occasions when I was sitting in a chair, Elizabeth happened to be practicing the manipulation of her wheelchair. (This wasn't really necessary—there were willing hands to place her wherever she wanted to be, but she was an independent soul, used to going under her own power.) She was inept, and the wheelchair was old and hard to maneuver. She bumped into my chair, lightly. It struck her as inordinately funny. "Accident! Collision! Put it in the Parker paper: Welsh bumped into Laird!"

The atmosphere of the women's ward was nothing if not relaxed. Visitors drifted in at all hours of the day and evening. Children of friends and relatives ran about freely. In the evening, one party of visitors set up a table where they played Chinese checkers or some similar game, while chatting with the patient. Most of the patients knew each other, most of them had been in and out of the hospital at least several times. There seemed to be a pattern. Women would come in for a couple of days of intravenous treatment with rest away from the heat, and good food. When they were somewhat built up, they would go back again to the conditions and surroundings that had dragged them down in the first place. At eight o'clock every evening a cart was brought in with large cold cans of a wide assortment of fruit juice and a stack of paper cups. It looked and tasted delicious, but even when I was free from nausea I limited myself to half a cup. I was afraid it would make my kidneys active during the night, and that, for reasons which I will explain, was a condition to be avoided.

Maternity was just down the hall. That was the busiest part of the hospital. It seemed that almost every night there were one or two births, and we could hear the cries of newborn babies. Occasionally there would be an emergency, a difficult birth. Nurses and aides wore anxious expressions, and everyone was concerned.

Once there must have been overcrowding in the maternity ward, for a screen was put around the empty bed at the end of the row and a secluded corner provided for a new mother and her baby. She was a white girl, married to a Mohave. The baby looked all Indian. In the morning she carried him about the ward to appropriate oohing and ahing. Then her young husband came for her, a tall young man in a big Stetson hat, and the family went home together.

An old, small black-and-white television set perched high on the wall at the far end of the ward. An aide turned it on the first thing in the morning and off at bedtime. The picture was probably not very clear at best and to me, merely a blur. It was set usually to a station that carried a series of ancient and inane reruns, and if by chance a snatch of news came on, someone immediately asked to have it changed. "I can't stand that stuff," was the standard comment. So during the month of August, 1974, I remained in ignorance of developments in Washington.

On Sunday afternoon just outside the hospital baseball was played. Everyone knew the players, those who could crowded to the windows to watch, and once an aide opened the door to the left of my bed and exchanged pleasantries, while a breath of not unwelcome outside air, hot but free of the closed-in hospital atmosphere, came into the room. (Not that there were bad odors. Come to think of it, these were remarkably lacking; but the air where sick people are has its own peculiar effluvia.) The air from out-of-doors smelled of dust and sprinklers on grass, and faintly (but I may have imagined this) of oleanders. The afternoon wore on, the ball game slowed down as the players loaded up on beer, and everyone was amused.

All in all, the ward was not an unpleasant place; but there was a circumstance that made it unpleasant for me. This was the attitude of two Mohave aides who did not share Elizabeth's tolerance. Their names were Pat and Pam, and I was never quite sure which was which. One was the girl who had sat by my bed the night I had the nightmare. It seemed that every day intensified her scorn for me. They cooed over Elizabeth in the next bed, brushing her hair, anticipating her every want, getting her up into the wheelchair (the ward only boasted one) and down again for a nap. I got attention only when I put on my light, and it was given with tight-lipped reluctance. I had been given to understand when I returned to the ward that no one was going to help me up onto a commode; I could use a bedpan or get to the bathroom under my own steam. To be fair, I believe I was occasionally taken to the toilet in the wheelchair, but this was done by some other aide. (Some of them were very kind indeed.) Understandably, I asked for the bedpan as little as possible when one of these girls was on duty. One night I had diarrhea, and put on my light about every half hour for awhile. The girl who brought the bedpan protested, "This is ridiculous! This is ridiculous!" Sometimes I happened to need something when the doctor was making his morning rounds. Pat (or Pam) would assist me reluctantly. "I wanted to go with the doctor," she would say. "You're keeping me from learning anything." Breaking away as soon as possible, she would hurry after the morning parade, arms swinging self-importantly, pausing to show off her efficiency in checking IVs. But the biggest complaint of this precious pair was that I was too heavy, I was straining their respective backs. I wanted desperately to practice with the walker. One day I made it over to a chair by the wall, a distance of about eight steps. But I sat too long, got dizzy, and just before I got back to the bed, started to collapse. Pam (or Pat) had hold of my arm. As I started to go down, she exclaimed, "Stand up, damn it! You can stand up if you want to—you walked over there all right!" Roughly, she half pulled, half pushed me back onto the edge of the bed.

This episode was the last straw for my unwilling helpers. They told the Head Nurse that I was entirely too heavy to manage, and she, doubtless anxious to keep peace among her

staff, decreed that there would be no more attempts at walking. If I sat in the chair again, I would be conveyed there by
a lift. This threat was never carried out, but afterwards I left
my bed only with the help of some of the more friendly aides
or one of the nurses who had managed so well in the private
room. One or the other of the friendly aides (I never asked
their tribe or tribes) was usually on duty in the morning, and
this meant I could visit the somewhat primitive bathroom, use
one of the toilets, and brush my dentures at the washstand. In
fairness I must admit that the unfriendly aides had some justi-
fication for complaining of my heaviness, if not for their rude-
ness. My body *was* deadweight most of the time, because I had
so little control over it. The woman in the bed opposite mine,
a Mohave, weighed two hundred and seventy-four pounds.
Fortunately, she was ambulatory, but I doubt if anyone would
have complained if she hadn't been. This woman, like many
of her tribe, reminded me of a Polynesian. (For what it's
worth, the Mohave have an origin myth about crossing great
waters.)

I had assumed my difficulties were due to my being white.
Not so, I later learned. I was the widow of a well-remembered
Chemehuevi, and old feuds are slow a-dying. (I wondered then
if Pat and Pam also gave a rough time to Willie Mike, an elderly
Chemehuevi in the hospital at that time.)

The attempt to amalgamate a comparatively few Chemehuevi with numerous Mohave, throw in a few Pima and Na-
vaho families, and label the mix the Colorado River Tribe, is
a noble example of governmental insensitivity.

From whatever complex roots of interracial or intertribal
tension these small sordid humiliations sprang, their cumula-
tive effect was to underscore my helplessness. My mind was
ever so gradually regaining its sharpness, my speech its clarity,
but mobility did not return. With no money of my own, no
income except small Social Security payments and a weekly
check of fifteen dollars from a friend I knew by correspondence only, and with no place to go after leaving the hospital,
despair assailed me if I permitted myself to think of the fu-

ture. I tried to live one day, one hour at a time. But there were periods when I could see nothing ahead except warehousing in some dreadful charity home for the aged. . . .

I had not felt very secure or very happy in my room in Georgia's mobile home in Chemehuevi Valley. Now I found myself remembering it wistfully. There had been at least a few of my books, some of which had been bedside companions for years; the well-worn red clothbound Bible, a book of Oriental psychology, paperbound books by Martin Buber and one by Alan Watts; also the books recently received in the mail, including biographies of Thomas Jefferson and Alexander the Great, and some gothic novels; also two large, well-printed paperbacks from the University of Utah Press, on the Numic myths gathered by Powell and Paiute ethnohistory, which had been recently loaned to me. All in all, a motley selection but I liked them.

And there had been my typewriter, sitting on the desk I had had so many years—now, alas, very wobbly, with one drawer missing and one leg propped up on a stack of science-fiction magazines. The damage had occurred when the truck bringing our heavier furniture from Los Angeles to the new home overturned in the desert.

This accident, which we referred to as The Wreck, is a story in itself. Georgia, from motives of misguided kindness and a very real need to save money, had employed a man from the Colorado River Reservation to drive a U-Haul truck while she went ahead with a loaded station wagon. The man she hired is a Sioux married to a Chemehuevi girl, a member of a family with whom Georgia was intimate. He had the reputation of being a hard drinker. But, Georgia said later, he had put up a fence for her and had been helpful in other ways, and she had persuaded herself that he had turned over a new leaf. He told her, quite truthfully, that the furniture was too heavy for him to handle by himself, and he would like to bring along a friend who did not drive but would help with the loading and unloading. She agreed to this, advanced money for the

gas, and departed for Chemehuevi Valley. There she waited.
And waited. Eventually she alerted the Highway Patrol. Two
days later the truck was located, overturned beside the highway south of Indio. Fragments of furniture, pieces of clothing,
and other items were scattered over the desert. Pieces of paper
were blowing about. (Many of my own manuscripts were destroyed or scattered in this mishap, including many if not all
of the original notes upon which I based *The Chemehuevis*.)
The driver and his companion had apparently vanished from
the earth. Later the driver sent word from Parker that he
would like the rest of his pay. Georgia sent word back that
she would kill him on sight. . . .

Looking back, I remembered my battered desk with affection. Even the fine pale dust sifting in and covering everything
now seemed tolerable. From my window there in the Chemehuevi Valley I could see, by standing and looking in both
directions, five houses, not all inhabited. Directly outside
there was the remnant, left by bulldozers, of a small wash,
now a miniature desert garden with rocky pavement intact,
a greasewood bush and several varieties of cholla. Tiny desert
chipmunks climbed on the fuzzy-looking one, the one covered
by minute vicious hooked thorns, and ran up and down its
branches as happily as squirrels scrambling from branch to
branch in an oak tree.

In the remote, heat-pale skies an occasional buzzard soared.
Sometimes from one to five wild burros took leisurely rolls in
the dust of the road, stood for a time in cool defiance of
Georgia's pack of small dogs, then ambled off towards the river.

The river was actually the northern end of Lake Havasu.
There was a large tule marsh, bright green when I came, rap-
idly browning when I left. On the near side of the marsh there
were trees—willows, and perhaps cottonwoods; I never went
close enough to distinguish. Occasionally a boat drifted along
the channel on the far side, the Arizona side, under high sand-
stone cliffs. These cliffs were desert beige in sunlight, black as
basalt when completely in shadow. Sometimes after days of
breathless calm a hot wind blew from across the scorching ex-

panse of the Sonoran Desert and dust stood tall against the mountains of Arizona. (In the old days, when there still remained remnants of the ancient culture, there lived a chief whose Chemehuevi name meant "Sand Standing.")

Now lying in my bed in Indian Hospital, I remembered all these things with nostalgia. Then, in spite of certain inconveniences and discomfort, in spite of my fears at being left alone while Georgia was away, I enjoyed a comparative freedom and could look forward to a brighter future. Now it seemed unlikely that I would ever again have a room that I could call my own. . . .

One evening Dan Eddy, a middle-aged man who, when a boy, had known George Laird, came to the hospital to call on George's widow. I had heard of him for years, but we had never before met. He is a son of "Doctor" Billy Eddy, the last of the great Chemehuevi shamans. The father was said to have possessed wonderful healing powers. He should have been very good indeed with burns and fevers, for his familiar or spirit-animal helper (or at least, one of his helpers) was the bat, who is unique in his power to produce great cold. When I went to Parker looking for informants in 1919—that was when I met George—Billy Eddy was mentioned as one of the older generation who were well-versed in the ancient lore and spoke Chemehuevi in its purest form. But I was discouraged from approaching him for it was said that he "did not talk to white people."* Now he had long since departed this world; not, I think for the Christian heaven, which would have been for him a place of torment, but for that Land of the Dead far

---

*I have been informed that in his later years Billy Eddy became more and more withdrawn, and did not talk much even with his own children. In the interim he must have mellowed somewhat, for Isabel Kelly interviewed him extensively. The information she records does not completely check with mine. She lists Ocean Woman as one of his helpers; my understanding is that Ocean Woman was never a shaman's familiar. Ocean Woman was the Creator. Anyone could petition her for help, but she did not come at the beck and call of any man.

off in the mysterious north, where his forebears awaited him. His son proved to be affable and self-possessed, a man of considerable presence.

Mr. Eddy said that after his visit with me he would go to the men's ward to visit Willie Mike, the elderly Chemehuevi, who had suffered a stroke some three months previously. "Willie gets pretty discouraged," he said, "but I try to drop by every now and then and cheer him up." Willie Mike had been an active and gregarious man all his life; confinement and immobility must have been hell for him.

Georgia was not doing well and never found herself able to make the trip to Parker. But on a red letter day Mary Mitchell drove over to see me. She brought Wayne, who kissed me and said, "How are you, Grandma?" and gave me a warm sense of family. Mary also brought not only my own toilet things but a comb and brush which she had purchased, and Wayne gave me a little mirror on a stand. Everyone exclaimed over how well I looked; but seeing myself for the first time since surgery, I was shocked at my ghastly pallor. My hair had grown to an awkward length, and I could not raise my arthritic arms to brush it properly. Mary promised to come back again and trim it, and she was as good as her word. This time she brought my checkbook, and on both occasions, mail. Now I had books from my book clubs. At last I had something to read. But one of the books was Stewart Alsop's *Stay of Execution*. I must have been in a peculiarly morbid and impressionable condition; perhaps my brush with the dark angel was still too recent, my escape not as complete as I had fancied. I found the book depressing—so depressing that I could not finish reading it. It must have been on her first visit that Mary Mitchell brought it, for I remember sending it back to Georgia, who also must have found it not very cheering.

On her second visit Mary's husband, Don, came with her, and they brought their beautiful, pathetic, five-year-old brain-damaged granddaughter. Little Tassa Trell's tiny arms and legs were helpless and undeveloped from lack of exercise, she could not hold her head erect; but her face was lovely, lighting up at intervals with a smile that could only be described as "angelic." I had the impression of imprisoned intelligence, unreachable and unable to communicate.

Another visitor was Pamela Munro, a graduate student of linguistics with whom I was committed to work on texts of the Chemehuevi myths recorded at the instigation of my first husband, John Peabody Harrington. When I had left him in 1920 I had left all this body of work behind, naively considering it to be his property, and after his death it was deposited in the anthropoligical archives of the Smithsonian Institution. Now I had the Xeroxed copies on which I had been working daily in the Chemehuevi Valley. (I remember that I had felt peculiarly sluggish on my birthday, and had told myself I would let "that one day" go past without touching the typewriter.) Now talking with Pamela I was overwhelmed with a realization of helplessness and isolation. Also I seemed to hear myself through her ears, and became shockingly aware of my blurred and dragging speech. I told her I feared I would never be able to collaborate; but Pamela heroically maintained that I would. To prove her sincerity, she then and there wrote a check for a hundred and fifty dollars. I have not yet done anywhere nearly enough in the way of collaboration to earn this amount; but I shall be eternally grateful for this gesture of confidence. It gave me one more anchor to sanity and hope.

The days went by, one much like another, except when visitors came. There was a gradually mounting sense of tension caused by my continued presence. Two of the more sympathetic nurses left, transferred to other posts—this was, you must remember, a U.S. Government institution. Although I felt gradually less ill, gradually stronger, I was having fewer opportunities to try to walk. I sensed that my prolonged stay, combined with my feud with Pat and Pam, was having a disruptive influence on the staff. The doctors might have been secretly on my side, but it meant a great deal to them to maintain harmony among the nursing personnel.

There were of course small pleasures and distractions. One morning two friendly aides happened to be on duty. They bustled up cheerfully, announcing that "they bet" they could get me into the bathroom and give me a shower. And that is exactly what they did, giving me a thorough shower and washing my hair, for the first time since I left Lake Havasu Community Hospital about a month before. Also there was a pleasant rapport with the young bearded student doctor. I called him "Dr. Livingstone, I presume" and shamelessly demanded small services from him—mostly, I believe, buying stamps and mailing letters. (Mary Mitchell had given me a coin purse with two dollars in change, and she must also have brought writing materials, for now with great difficulty I was beginning to write—mostly checks for books that had come while I was ill.) Sometimes when I beckoned "Dr. Livingstone" he would spread his hands helplessly and gesture that he had other duties; but when he could, he came in and talked and I felt that he enjoyed my company as I enjoyed his. He brought me a well-worn paperback copy of *Catch 22*, which it happened that I had not read—and which now, for some reason or other, failed to hold my attention.

Dr. Bertman went away for a few days, attending some sort of convention. When he came back he told me he had been giving serious consideration to my situation. Like Dr. Stoker before him, he assured me that he had no intention of turning me out with nowhere to go. I expressed my utter horror of a certain sort of nursing home. He said not to fear for a moment that I would be sent to such a place. He was looking into the situation, he would find a place where there was a resident therapist, where I could be active and have help in learning to walk again. I told him cautiously that I now had enough in the bank to pay three hundred dollars towards care, for one month only. But I couldn't obligate my social security, because I still owed doctors' bills to the staff of Lake Havasu Community Hospital, and even something to Palomar Memorial. With equal caution Dr. Bertman implied rather than stated it might not be necessary for me to pay anything.

Vi Jackson now entered the picture, a pretty, thin, pale brown woman, Apache with a mixture of two other tribes.

She was the social worker and Mabel Axtell's good friend. They went horseback riding together, disregarding the merciless heat of late afternoon.

All too quickly—for again I dreaded change—I was informed that Dr. Bertman had located just the place for me. It was the Golden Mesa Nursing and Convalescent Home in Phoenix, not a charity place, not inexpensive. But I was not to offer to try to pay anything. Because I was a patient in Indian Hospital, the Public Health Service would pick up the entire tab.

"For how long?" I asked.

"Why, for the rest of your life if you want to stay," Vi responded brightly.

I literally felt my heart sink. Somewhere in my mind an iron door clanged shut.

Mabel said it wouldn't be like Indian Hospital; there would surely be a telephone in every room. This was reassuring. It had been close to forty years since we installed the primitive old telephone on the bedroom wall in Poway, and since then I had never been without one. But when she added that I would have the companionship of people my own age, my heart sank again. I thought I knew what that would be like; fortunately for my peace of mind, I could not even imagine it.

I had now a coin purse, comb and brush, checkbook, and glasses; but nothing to carry these things in. I asked Mabel Axtell for an old handbag, something that she would never want back. She gave me one that had seen better days but was still serviceable. She also loaned me a case in which to carry my books. This was Bureau of Indian Affairs property and I was supposed to return it at my convenience, but to date I have not done so.

PART II
Limbo

1

It was standard practice to transfer patients from Indian Hospital in Parker to Phoenix by air, and I rather looked forward to the trip. But I was told in this case we were to go by ambulance. There were two of us going; Willie Mike was to be placed in the same Nursing Home. He had had no therapy to help him regain some use of himself after his stroke, and it was said that he had an enormous bedsore.

The fifth of September was the time set for our departure. When the aides came in to prepare me for departure, one of them remarked, "Uncle Willie's all ready to go." The other laughed. "He wouldn't be so anxious if he knew what he was going to." I too had begun to be anxious to go. Now, overhearing, I felt again that cold sinking of the heart that had followed Vi's words, "the rest of your life."

Willie was already in the ambulance when I was placed beside him. His strong old face, dark and deeply lined, had not a sign of animation and he looked neither to the right nor to the left. My heart went out to him. I tried to say, "I met you once at Faythe Brown's," but for some reason I could not think of "Brown" and said "Taylor" instead. He gave no sign at all of having heard. Perhaps he did not hear, perhaps he was only vaguely conscious of the white woman muttering gibberish that did not concern him. For me this was the first of many attempts at friendliness when I seemed to address a stone wall. In the experience I was to have with other "inmates" of the Nursing Home I never knew whether the person spoken to was stone deaf, mentally incompetent, or merely uninterested in replying.

It took us about three hours to reach Phoenix. I was in better shape now than on the other ambulance ride from Lake Havasu City to Parker. Over my green nightgown I wore the long muumuu that Georgia had sent me by Mary. I had some small luggage with me. I now had a handbag, my watch, and best of all, my glasses. I was stronger now, better able to hold the ambulance curtains open a slit; and the desert was distinct to my view. I found myself wondering how far George's ancestors had roamed in this direction and what the old place-names had been. At best, I am poor at geography. I had on record many Chemehuevi place-names for Arizona, but now, still handicapped by mental fuzziness, I could not orient myself. I knew that I was measurably improved, however, because when we stopped at gas stations and the ambulance was left untended for a few minutes, I no longer feared that I would die of heat.

Comparatively pleasant though the journey was, I knew that each moment it lasted took me farther from friends and relatives, farther from anyone who could possibly know or care about what happened to me. I knew one family in Phoenix but could not remember their address. Although we were good friends, my confused mind could scarcely be sure of their name. Was it Hunter and did they live on Anderson Street? Or was it the other way around? Were they actually in Phoenix or Tempe? I could mentally see Phoenix on her letters—but could I be sure? Fighting my way out of the fog by sheer effort of will, I still had a long way to go.

Then we were in the city, then turning into a driveway flanked by conventional oases of shrubbery. The name of the place was Golden Mesa Nursing and Convalescent Home, but the word "Mesa" was misleading. It proved to be a large one-story building situated on perfectly level land. The name was painted in large letters on a sign—I am sure it was a large rectangular sign, but my memory insists on picturing it as an arch. For a moment I thought it might as well have read: "Abandon hope all ye who enter here"; then my mind fastened on the word "Convalescent" and I felt faintly reassured. Convalescents are people who are expected to get well, who have a place in the world to which they will return. But where would my place be?

The ambulance backed up to wide glass doors opening on a cheerful entrance hall with bouquets of artificial flowers. I was wheeled down one corridor and Willie Mike down another. I never saw him again. All my inquiries were in vain. Nurses didn't know just whom I meant, even the kind and competent therapist couldn't place him. It wasn't till I met Rosita, the pleasant, low-voiced Apache girl who was the Bureau of Indian Affairs social worker for Indians confined in nursing homes in that area, that I learned Willie Mike's fate. He had died "of pneumonia" one week after admission. If that long journey to Phoenix had been dismaying to a person like myself, accustomed to moving from place to place, with what despair it must have stricken him! He had been all his life an active man, free to move about among his own people. With his keen Indian sense of territoriality, he must have realized all too clearly that he was being carried farther and farther from all that constituted his life! And at the end he was shut away in a stuffy room with strange, sick, or mentally incompetent white men. "Pneumonia" was as good a diagnosis as any; he had simply exercised the age-old prerogative of his people of turning away from an untenable situation.

I was taken to a narrow, dark room with four beds in it. This, I learned later, was known as The Ward. It was as different as possible from the light and lively eight-bed ward at Indian Hospital. I was placed in the bed nearest to the door. At the other end of the room the curtains were drawn over the single window. The beds were in a row down one side of the room and the entrance and bathroom, and a chair in which visitors (or sometimes patients) could sit, occupied the other side. It wasn't a large room and the bathroom was only halfway down it. One of my first thoughts was that I could perhaps walk that far; and if not now, soon.

Apprehension, however, was the dominant emotion. There was something terribly ominous about being dumped into a hospital bed in this stale, half-dark room with other women who did not—or perhaps could not—take any interest in their surroundings.

I clutched my purse for reassurance. The attendant told me to dump out its contents. She was a large, husky young black woman with a pretty, rather pleasant face and powerful forearms. The old-fashioned adjective "strapping" would describe her. She had the authoritarian, no-nonsense manner of a person who has dealt too much with the mentally incompetent and the physically helpless. I felt a desperate need to establish a friendly relationship, but I could not without protest part with the meager—but oh, so precious!—contents of my handbag.

I said, "There is really nothing of value in here to anyone but me. I just have less than two dollars in a coin purse and my checkbook."

I was told firmly, "I have to make an inventory and you have to sign it. Then everything has to be locked up in the office." She glanced at my wrist and added, "And your watch too."

Without a watch, what would there be in this dim room to mark the passage of time? Desperation made me bold and, I think, persuasive. I said, "It's just a Timex, a cheap one at that. Please let me keep it. I'll sign a statement that I take full responsibility."

Amazingly, the woman relented. I was emboldened to say, "The checkbook is no good to anyone else. I need it to pay some bills. And I have to write a lot of letters. I really need the change for stamps." . . . I smiled and asked, "What's your name? I would like to know what to call you."

"Lois," the big girl said. She looked at me curiously. She was not used to articulate patients. Her manner became less impersonal. She said, "You can keep the stuff for now. You'll have to talk to the nurse about that checkbook."

I relaxed. One hurdle at least successfully taken. When the dinner tray came in, I praised it inordinately. The portions were small, which—at the time—impressed me favorably. There was spinach, canned of course; some kind of meat, which miraculously was not too loathsome; and also a small mound of mashed potatoes, unseasoned and watery, mixed up from the cheapest sort of precooked potato. I put salt and pepper on them, and also used the small pat of margerine with them instead of on my bread, and ate perhaps a third of this concoction, and all the spinach, and a few bites of the anonymous piece of meat. Lois removed the muumuu and let me remain in bed. I was exhausted by the morning's experiences and made no objection to the bedpan.

The other nurses' aides were shifted constantly, but for the daytime shift Lois was always in charge of The Ward, and the room next to it, in which, she said, were "two colored ladies." I saw these black women later in the dining room and at church services, where their tears flowed and their "Yes, Lords" and "Amens" punctuated the address or harangue, depending upon the visiting ministers. Both were in wheelchairs. One was Mrs. Brown, I never knew the other's name. Except that one was darker than the other, they were remarkably similar in appearance. Their scant, crisp, graying hair was drawn back in tight knots. They had long faces with full lips, the lower lip thrust out, almost pendulous. Seen in profile, these faces were ancient African masks. Lois said they gave her no trouble. And she was kind enough to put me in the same category.

This couldn't be said of the Italian woman in the next bed. She persistently refused all food. When I first came, Lois tried to coax her to eat; after a day or two she simply placed the meal before her and took it away when the other trays were collected. I feared she would starve to death before my eyes.

But after several days she had visitors, a man and wife, who assured me that this rejection of food was a normal aftereffect of the type of surgery she had had—what type I have no idea—or perhaps of medication. She had been through it all before, they said, and would get her appetite back in time. Meantime, I don't know what she lived on. She was not given intravenous feeding, as she would have been had she been a patient in the supposedly primitive and ill-equipped Indian Hospital. In one of the talks which Lois and I occasionally had, I spoke of the great need for patience in dealing with the old and the sick. "I know it," Lois said, "but sometimes I don't have it. I sure don't have it with that woman."

One day Lois got Mrs. Gallardo (whatever her name was, I am sure it began with G) up into the chair, and left her there. Soon the woman became tired. There was no call bell that she could reach. She began to cry, and it distressed me terribly. Presently I became inured to "Please somebody help me!" at all hours of the day and night, and no longer expected anyone to pay any attention. Later, much later, when a nurses' aide was doing some routine task in the room where I was, I said something about the dismal cries of some other patient echoing down the corridor. The answer was, "She takes on that way all the time." Now the Italian woman's distress moved me terribly. I knew, or thought I knew, what it was like from the few times I had been left overlong in a chair at Indian Hospital. I may have put on my light. Somebody—it may have been Lois—came in, but did nothing. The Italian woman yelled imprecations. The institution would be sued. In a few days her nephew was coming from Chicago. He had influence. He would make them sorry. He was going to take her home with him. This, too, soon became an old story. Son or daughter or nephew or sister was always coming next week (or tomorrow or in the spring). If the patient was very old, very senile, it would be mother who was coming to take her home.

Eventually, about three-thirty or four, the aides on the three-to-eleven shift came in and put Mrs. Gallardo to bed.

Then her tray was brought in and set before her and presently taken away untouched.

The other two women in The Ward were both named Mary. Neither one ever spoke. The one nearest the window was a "feeder"—food that had been put through a blender had to be put into her mouth, small bites at a time. The other one had to eat pureed food, but she could lift the spoon to her mouth, though sometimes she needed encouragement. One afternoon an old gentleman wheeled himself into The Ward and parked by her bed. He launched into a long harangue which, if you just caught a word now and then, sounded like the speech of an intelligent man, but more closely heard proved to be all sound and fury. There were references to Japan, earthquakes, Alaska, and long-past political events, all jumbled together with never a completed sentence. The old woman, propped up in bed, scanty hair pulled back from her forehead, toothless and expressionless, gave no sign that she was aware of his presence. I later learned that they were husband and wife. Their name was Dole, or something like that. Mr. Dole placed himself in the front row at every religious service, of whatever denomination; but I was told that he was no longer allowed near the bookshelves in the dining room, because one day he had gone in and torn up all the Bibles.

Lois explained to me quite kindly, "Once I get you up, you have to stay till the aides come to put you to bed. When I make that bed there's no getting back into it. Is that perfectly clear?"

"Perfectly clear," I said, "but I'm not used to sitting up long at a time—could you get me up kind of late?"

She goodnaturedly agreed, and thereafter I sat in the chair after the midday meal, which was the main meal of the day.

But one day the edict went out that everyone able to feed themselves must eat dinner in the dining room. From somewhere Lois came up with a red and black plaid cotton dress that fastened down the front. It occurred to me that it might have belonged to some patient who had died. It did not fit very well and I don't remember what was used for a slip—possibly the dress went on over the hospital nightgown. Lois wheeled me into the dining room and promised to come for me afterwards. My shoulders hurt, the muscles of my upper arms were painful, and I was ridiculously weak. I despaired of ever being able to learn to manipulate a wheelchair, but was told that I would have to, the exercise would be good for me.

I don't remember much about that meal. I was already thoroughly disillusioned about the food, which seemed to grow worse by the day. There were a number of tables seating four, and longer tables at the ends of the room. I tried to introduce myself to the other three at my table, but met no response. Mr. and Mrs. Dole sat side by side at one of the long tables. He was talking, she looked neither to the right nor to the left. What mentality she had was focused on slowly spooning up food from the three small metal bowls in front of her.

There I saw the two old black women, Mrs. Brown and her roommate. There were three Mexican women, one was a Mrs. Moreno, who walked quite well with the aid of a walker. A canvas bag was attached to her walker, and in it she secreted slices of bread that had not been unwrapped and little unused packages of sugar. I think she had been a hearty, hard-working woman, and the amount of food she was served fell short of her requirements. She had a proud, beautiful face and an erect carriage. I did not speak to her then, but later we became quite well acquainted. Her husband had been a miner, and she may have said he was killed in the mine. They had raised a family of children, and I cannot understand why she was not with them. Possibly she was recuperating from hospitalization. The other Mexican women were less competent, physically or mentally.

When the meal was over, there was a general rush to leave the dining room. Wheelchairs collided, and no one would yield. Sometimes a person at one table would want to leave before the person sitting back to back at the next table was ready to leave, and his exit would be blocked. Or both would want to leave at the same time, and there would not be enough cooperation for either one to get out. Finally the room was clear of all except a few who were waiting for assistance. No one helped me, and painfully I got myself into the corridor. Then Lois came along and took pity on me.

Because of the timeless monotony of institutional life, I have forgotten how long I was in The Ward. One week? Ten days? Two weeks? I know that I became accustomed to the routine, and, if not attached, at least accustomed to Lois, so that I no longer feared her. Of the various pairs of aides who came in the afternoon to put me to bed, I remember one very distinctly. It consisted of Hattie and Consuelo. Hattie was black and very pretty. Her hair was cut very short, like a crisp, closely fitting black cap, and in her pierced ears she wore tiny coral earrings. Although very strong and very quick, she limped. One leg was obviously an inch or two shorter than the other. Her infirmity was never mentioned. But later I was in a room where one of the patients who had never noticed her limp before suddenly became aware of it.

"How did you hurt yourself?" she asked.

"I didn't," Hattie responded briefly.

With the querulous persistence and lack of tact of the aged, the woman persisted until she elicited the information that Hattie "was born that way."

Consuelo also was young and pretty. The two aides appeared to be congenial and worked together well, but their temperaments were as different as possible. The Mexican aide bubbled over with an outrageous ebullience. Her mouth was as busy as her hands. She chanted the bones of the body and to which one each was connected, naming them (correctly or incorrectly, I haven't the faintest idea) in a way that made it sound like high comedy. In no time I knew that she was married, had two children, and where she lived. But I never learned very much about Hattie.

After my first visit to the dining room, I must have brought some means of persuasion to bear upon Lois, for I certainly don't remember going every day or being required to sit up

for a very long time without a rest—and yet I'm quite sure
Lois didn't break her rule and put me back to bed.

However that may be, I know that I was in bed in a sitting
position on the Saturday or Sunday when Mrs. Gallardo's
friends came to see her and chatted with me a few minutes,
reassuring me about her condition. They told me, in response
to my question, that there was not the slightest chance of
her nephew coming out from Chicago, either to visit her or
to remove her. This conversation went on within a few feet
of her bed; either she was deaf or so self-absorbed as to be
indifferent.

I was also sitting with the top portion of my bed cranked
up when Deacon North came to give Mrs. Gallardo the Sacrament and to remind her that Mass would be said on the third
Saturday of the month. Mr. North was a tall man, and inordinately fat, especially around the hips and thighs where most
men tend to be less heavy. Later I learned that he was a kind
and admirable person, married, with two children; a lay worker, devoted to the church.

I don't remember what I read in The Ward, yet I must have
had something to read or I would have gone mad. The light
was uniformly dim—I don't remember switching on the light
at the head of my bed, though surely one was there. Fortunately, my eyes do not require a great deal of light. I vaguely
recall that I prevailed on Lois or Hattie or Consuelo—I think
it was Consuelo, though she was always chattering, and the
aides on this shift were always rushing—to give me a book
from the case I had brought from Parker.

I learned that I was supposed to have my own nightgowns.
At any rate, most private patients had, and for some reason
I was, as I was later informed, classified as a private patient.
However, the Home had plenty of those dreadful open-behind
hospital nightgowns, so I didn't worry about that. I would al-
so be required to furnish my own lotion and dusting powder,
but I had a supply left over from Lake Havasu Community
Hospital. And I had held onto my precious checkbook.

Since the curtains were always drawn, I was glad to be in the bed nearest the door. At the end of the room next to the darkened window I would have felt immured in an autistic world, where the bright spark of intellect I had fought so hard to maintain might finally have flickered out. In that situation I might even have welcomed the ordeal of the dining room. As it was, I could look a little way down the corridor and there was a usually welcome sense of activity. A little quiet, however, would have been more welcome in the small hours of the night and early in the morning. There was a broom closet a few feet beyond the always open door. From it very early in the morning a man addressed as "Joe" removed housekeeping utensils with a great clatter, and there was much calling back and forth. In this place no nurse or attendant ever made the slightest effort to lower their voice. Shift changes were noisy, coffee breaks marked by unmodulated chatter. Perhaps they felt that some of the patients were so noisy and most of them so deaf that it made no difference. More probably this lack of consideration was just a symptom of the conviction—unvoiced and unrecognized—that the old and the mentally incompetent are not entirely human.

I don't remember a visit from the therapist during this period; certainly I would remember walking with her assistance. Perhaps she was ill or on vacation.

2

One morning after I had become accustomed to the routine of The Ward, and even felt that I had established a sort of rapport with Lois, a nurse hurried in and announced that I was to be moved to a better room. There was another patient there who was "more like" me, and whose company I would enjoy. It would be a much better situation for me.

My few belongings were collected, I was got up into a wheelchair and wheeled out the door. We turned a corner by a nurses' station and proceeded up a long corridor. My worry—in such a situation I could always find something to worry about—was that I was being taken so far from the dining room that I could never travel the distance by myself if everyone refused to push me. The corridor was painted green and had a blond wooden railing at a height where it could be gripped by the occupant of a wheelchair. We went up a very small ramp. At the top of it there was another nurses' station to my left and what I was informed was the "TV Room" (more accurately, the smoking room, though it was never called that) to my right. A very short distance farther on we turned left into a well-lighted room with curtains open to reveal sky and greenery, the low wall around the Nursing Home, and beyond it a road with houses on the opposite side backed by tall trees.

56

There were three beds in this room and they were as close together as those in The Ward, but for some reason it seemed infinitely less crowded. "The lady in the middle bed" had moved (at first I took this as a euphemism for "died," but later I heard that she had been taken by her relatives to a greatly inferior nursing home in another town), and the beneficent authorities had decided that I would be good company for Mrs. Kramer. The nurse introduced us.

Mrs. Kramer was sitting in a large, upholstered armchair in the corner next to the window. (It was a chair that could be electrically operated at the touch of a button, lifting the occupant to an almost standing position or gently lowering her when she wished to sit down. It was, of course, Mrs. Kramer's private property.) My impression was of daintiness, courtesy, and—best of all—intelligence. Here was someone who could take part in an intelligent conversation. I must have been a frightful mess, wearing either the muumuu which was many sizes too large and drooped off my left shoulder or the too-tight rather horrible black and red plaid, with a revolting expanse of bare leg between its hem and my shabby black shoes. My hair was thin and straight and wild and I had seen when I left Parker what my face looked like. It didn't faze this gentle lady. She told me her name was Florence and when I told her mine, repeated it accurately, which was enough to raise her in my estimation. Then she introduced me to the woman nearest the door, "Laura, this is Carobeth, our new roommate." The introduction met with the blank reception to which I had become accustomed. This woman's name, as I soon learned from her midnight soliloquies, was Lura, not Laura—"L-U-R-A, Lura, that's my name. Why does everybody have to call me Laura? I wouldn't *be* named Laura." She and I were to exchange words in the future, but she didn't waste speech on social amenities.

Florence was a woman who had been beautiful in youth and was still beautiful in old age and infirmity. (I regret that I must use the past tense in speaking of her, not as a literary device but because she died in August, 1975. We might never have seen one another again, yet I feel a lasting sense of loss.

Her death preceeded that of her husband by only eight
months.) She had been in Golden Mesa for well over a year
(or was it for over two years?) and before that had spent
a long time in and out of various hospitals for various and
painful operations, including total replacements of both hips
and the removal of an eye because of glaucoma. Her hands,
which had once been beautiful, were terribly deformed by
rheumatoid arthritis. She had come to Golden Mesa unable to
feed herself. Now, through the kind offices of the therapist,
she could grasp a slender plastic glass in her left hand and use
a large spoon to manage cut-up food. She remained in so much
pain that every breath (sometimes even when she was asleep)
was accompanied by a small, almost inaudible sound of pain
—not a groan, not a whimper, not a stifled cry; just a minute,
involuntary (and I am quite sure unconscious) protest in-
duced by constant, all but unbearable torture.

Florence's impaired vision did not permit her to lose herself in the printed word, as I did. Each morning she read with
effort from two small pamphlets containing prayers for the
sick. And at night she clasped her rosary.

Yet this was a woman whose presence would brighten any
room. She was invariably cheerful, kind, uncomplaining; and
she had a nice sense of humor and an even nicer sense of courtesy. As the days passed I learned that it was her habit to address all the dreary inhabitants of that place brightly, regard-
less of lack of response. And, amazingly, there sometimes was
a response from the most unlikely source. Moreover, she was
attractive and took pride in her appearance. She had a closet
full of dainty short nightgowns (which doubled as slips during
the day—none of us wore more than two garments) and pretty,
summery dresses, and each day selected with care what she
wished to wear. There was no nurses' aide so churlish that she
would not brush and press the wave into her abundant, graying hair.

Every day, at a little past noon, Mrs. Kramer's husband
came to see her. To his family he was known as "Mike,"
though that wasn't his name. A big, competent, kindly man,

utterly devoted, he spent a good deal of time doing little services for his wife which in their haste or incompetence the attendants had neglected. I don't know if he had ever served in the Navy, but he had the ritual neatness of an ex-Navy man. Every day he wiped clean the top of her nightstand and the adjustable table on which meals were served. In the evening, unless he was seriously under the weather, he came back for another visit. Often at midday he brought a hamburger and milkshake to supplement the institutional fare; and occasionally grapes, which to my delight were shared with me.

Mr. Kramer was retired, living (by preference) alone in an apartment. He was his wife's senior by a year—I think their respective ages were seventy-three and seventy-four. They had been married to each other for most of their lives and had two children: a boy in Hawaii and a daughter, married but without children—they would have made wonderful parents, Florence commented wistfully—living on the edge of a suburban golf course. After Mrs. Kramer had been taken to visit this home, she remarked that it was "like something out of *House & Garden*."

Every Wednesday Jeanette came into town with her husband and spent the whole day at Golden Mesa. She did her mother's nails, read letters, shared pleasant gossip of family and friends. Wednesday was a day to look forward to, and soon I too began to enjoy it. Jeanette brought me copies of her husband's *The Wall Street Journal*, and was herself a reassurance that a world still existed beyond the low stucco wall that enclosed this institution.

Because she had a family who kept careful watch over her and were probably not without influence—they would, at the least, have been capable of influencing public opinion—Florence Kramer was able to assert her individual preferences rather more than most of the patients. Although she was not technically a "feeder," and thereby according to the rules should have gone to the dining room, she flatly refused. She did not care to expose herself to the humiliation of struggling through a meal in public. And besides, she would have been unable to transport herself and that would have made more work for the attendants. Lura, on the other hand, zipped about in her wheelchair with gusto. She was, however, the most stubborn individual I ever came in contact with, and she adamantly refused to go to the dining room. (Towards the end of my stay she changed her mind and began to appear for the noonday meal fairly often. When I spoke to her about it, she flared up: "I guess I'll go if I want to; I do what I want to do.") Perhaps with two persons in the room refusing the trip, it seemed rather pointless to force the third. The upshot was that I generally, though not always, escaped. Once when a nurse came in and urged that I "really should go," I reminded her that I was still nauseated at mealtimes and had to take "antinausea pills." (When I left I learned that these tiny pink and white capsules, prescribed by Dr. Bertman in Indian Hospital, were Benadryl, a very mild tranquilizer. Their effect was probably more psychosomatic than biochemical.) At any rate, it came about that we three were generally in our room for the noon meal. Florence and I made it something of a social occasion. We commiserated with each other on the quality of the food, which was, with few exceptions, awful. Sometimes Florence did not eat at all—but then she could rely on her husband to see that she was fed. I ate doggedly, whether or not I liked the fare, determined to regain my strength. Lura ate as though she were alone in the room. She usually cleaned her tray, eating methodically, with little smacking noises of appreciation, even while she muttered occasional complaints about cold coffee or—very rarely—some dish she didn't like.

In Room 36 our days began sometime around six-thirty when a nurses' aide opened the curtain and let in the bright desert morning. If she was an aide we liked, Florence and I would ask eagerly, "Are you our nurse for today?" If she really liked us, she answered, "I hope so." But usually she simply said, "The schedules haven't been posted yet." And perhaps added acidly, "And when they are posted, I suppose they'll change them half a dozen times." This was one of the continual plaints of patients and aides: No attendant knew where she was going to be from one day to the next, no one stayed in one place long enough to work out a routine that suited both herself and the occupants of the room under her care. But a few of the aides we were glad not to have regularly, and breathed a sigh of relief when we knew they were to work elsewhere. Not that anyone was actually cruel or even blatantly incompetent; but there are varying minor degrees of discourtesy and neglectfulness, keenly felt by the helpless.

The aides were all "girls," in institutional usage, no matter what their age. Many of them were quite young women, newly married or expecting to be married, or young married women with children, concerned about baby-sitters. The oldest of them was Jewell, in her early fifties, unmarried. She spoke with the unmistakable accents of Oklahoma. Jewell was efficient and usually kind, but always rushed. She moved in an awkward, forward-leaning trot, always pressured, always put-upon, complaining that she answered the other aides' lights but they never answered hers. Jewell had no skills or patience with hair. She brushed it straight back with hard strokes, and trimmed fingernails (judging from what she once did to mine) straight across and down to the quick.

Nonetheless Jewell was one of our favorites. Florence especially liked her. It seemed that Mr. Kramer once or twice encountered her going into the same apartment building where he put in his solitary hours looking forward to the day that Florence should be well enough to "come home"; and when that happy day came, Florence intended to ask Jewell to visit them. There was a rapport between them. I think Jewell even moderated her harsh strokes when she did Florence's hair, although nothing would ever make her a hairdresser. If it was Jewell who pulled open the curtains, she almost invariably handed each of us a warm washcloth, a nicety about which most of the "girls" never troubled themselves. (But once or twice she said gruffly, "I got no time, I got too many patients to take care of this morning." Or again, "They got no washrags this morning.")

Jewell had her patients' interests at heart. She made haste each morning that she was assigned to us to get fairly decent wheelchairs for Lura and me. (Florence had her own privately owned wheelchair, stored in the closet across the hall. It had small wheels—perhaps this kind is a little easier for someone else to maneuver, and Florence's crippled hands could never be used for self-propulsion. For those who depended on institutionally owned chairs, there were never enough in a fair state of repair to go around.) Jewell was beautifully impartial in finding a wheelchair for Lura, but she couldn't abide Lura's habits. Lura kept her bedpan in bed with her. (She crooned to it in the night, calling it her "friend," her "pal.") After the late-night "girls" had looked in for the last time about 6:00 a.m. and had put the other bedpans away, Lura invariably used hers and set it on the portable table at the foot of the bed, which would presently be pushed into place across the bed so that her breakfast tray could be placed upon it. And once, after our midday dinner trays had been taken away, instead of wheeling herself into the toilet, as she was perfectly capable of doing, Lura extracted her bedpan from the nightstand where it had been put away for the day, and with that monkey-like agility that we wondered at and envied, climbed from the wheelchair to the bed and squatted upon it, never troubling to draw the curtains. She always resented it in the evening when I partially drew my curtains in the vain hope of escaping her comments about my reading habits, saying she liked fresh air and I was blocking it off. Florence, bred in the midwestern upper-middle-class tradition of refinement, suffered agonies of embarrassment for fear that Mike would come in at this juncture—or that the bedpan, though no longer in use, would be sitting unemptied and in plain view. Fortunately—and it was unusual for this time of day—someone did come in and empty it before his arrival. This was the type of behavior on Lura's part that shook Jewell's composure. Her standard remark upon entering the room in the morning was, "I'm gittin' sick of a pan of pee starin' me in the face." Even as she protested she was emptying it. And afterwards she always took time to wash her hands—something the other attendants rarely troubled to do.

Each morning, after the first minimal attention to our needs, Jewell (or whoever the "girl" in attendance was) went out. There would be a brief hiatus, filled with loud complaints from the corridor about the schedule and nurses' voices giving instructions that would routinely be disregarded: "I want everybody—I mean *everybody*—who doesn't have a bowel movement to have an enema. I don't want anymore of this going three or four days and then vomiting. It is our profession to care for people." Then a creaking and a rattling of crockery would announce the arrival of the breakfast trays. The "girl" for the day would crank up the heads of our beds so that we could sit up (but not Lura's bed—she sat bolt upright and did not permit anyone to tamper with her bed). Then the aide would wheel the bed tables into place and bring in our trays. Florence needed to have her milk and coffee poured into slim plastic glasses which she was able to grasp and her food cut into small bites. These services were performed graciously or reluctantly, depending upon mood and the pressure of work. But they were always performed; the care of "feeders" and partial "feeders" was an inescapable duty.

Breakfast was invariably cold, except for the coffee, which might be lukewarm. The meal consisted of approximately three tablespoonsful of an unsalted, thin, farina-type gruel, with a glass of milk which could be drunk (I never drank it) or poured on the gruel. There were also scrambled powdered eggs, very dry and imperfectly mixed, with streaks and lumps of bright yellow, accompanied by a tough slice of toast, too cold to melt the single pat of butter, and a little jelly in a square plastic container. Sometimes there would be a prepackaged waffle, scorched but now cold, and syrup instead of jelly. And occasionally a very cold, very stale sweet roll instead of eggs and toast. Sunday mornings the meal was served on a paper plate. When I first came we once had a small sausage and twice a single strip of bacon, but these expensive luxuries were soon discontinued. The breakfast juice seemed usually to be an imperfectly dissolved powdered beverage. Very rarely we were served a glass of delicious pink grapefruit juice, surely donated; and prune juice was provided when requested.

Sooner or later, after breakfast trays were removed, our attendant would get us up for the day. Now I was torn by one of those deep concerns over trivia which typically afflict persons dependent upon the services of others. I wanted to be got up "sooner" because I frequently had urgent need to use the toilet; and "later" because the longer I could stay in bed, the shorter would be my often agonizing "sit" in the wheelchair. Among the nurses' aides it was an invariable rule that "their" patients would not lie down again after the bed was neatly made. Ambulatory patients (or agile ones, like Lura) continually disregarded this decree; but those who could not climb from chair to bed had perforce to obey it. The day after I was moved to Room 36 I sat in my wheelchair for seven hours continuously. My back felt as if it would break in two, for I had not since my surgery been up for more than an hour at a time, and that not on any regular basis. I turned and twisted, bent forward and leaned back without relief. Not much later I asked for and obtained a pillow to sit on and another for my back. These furnished some relief. Also I was gradually growing stronger. I learned that by great insistence I could get a "girl" to place the call button where I could reach it, and occasionally someone would answer it and assist me into the bathroom. Also once in a great while, if the walker was left within reach and if the wheelchair had good brakes or could be braced in position, I, greatly daring, stood up and made my precarious way to the toilet. These changes of position helped enormously. But once there was some emergency and the "girls" on the evening shift did not arrive to bed us down for the night till after eight o'clock. Florence and I collapsed with fatigue.

The process of being got up consisted of being assisted to the bathroom to use the commode, then a brief and cursory wash-up, most of which I was expected to do for myself. These activities were frequently delayed until our "girl" for the day could secure a combination commode/bathchair to place over the toilet bowl for those of us who were unable to sit on a toilet seat of the usual height. There were not enough of these commodes to go around, and the search was sometimes long and vocal, accompanied by accusations and recriminations. One particular commode was in better condition and easier to wheel than the others, and therefore was much in demand, especially when the patient was to be given a shower. "Who stole my Cadillac?" was a demand frequently heard.

After ablutions, the patient was allowed to choose what she would wear. Florence was always definite and firm. "The blue nightgown—no, the pale blue with the lace. And the striped dress with puff sleeves." She was not fussy, not querulous, but she knew her own mind. She clearly visualized the nightie doubling as under slip that would best suit in length and neck contour the dress she wished to wear. And of the dress, she often said to me happily, "Jeanette made this for me." I soon was able to add a few garments to my own wardrobe.

For Lura the getting up process was somewhat different. As soon as the breakfast tray was removed, she was in a fever to leave her bed. If her wheelchair was not yet brought in or had been placed out of reach, she fretted and fumed. Since she could propel herself into the bathroom and could dress herself unaided, and since the aides were rushed and overworked and didn't wish to struggle with her, whoever was on duty usually handed her her clothes without argument. She had one black slip (she said another black one and a rose-

colored one had been stolen), and a few dresses, none of them
washable. She preferred a certain black and white one, which
she wore day after day. On shower mornings she generally said
with counterfeit reasonableness, "I'm taking cold. I don't think
I'll have a shower today." Consequently her luxuriant, shoul-
der-length dark iron-gray hair hung limp and greasy. (Florence
said it was "such pretty hair when it was cared for.") She had
to be reminded to run a comb through it—a large black comb
sequestered somewhere among the jumble of old letters,
papers, tracts, purloined ashtrays, and other knickknacks that
filled her purse to bursting. (When she could not immediately
locate this comb, Lura always called out that it had been
stolen while she slept.) As soon as her sketchy toilet was completed, Lura climbed into her wheelchair and propelled herself
out the door, exclaiming with impatience if a clothes hamper,
housekeeper's cart, or another chair blocked her exit.

When I had watched this process a few mornings, I asked
Florence, "Why is she always in such a hurry?"

"Didn't you know?" Florence replied. "She wants to be in
time for her cigarette."

Cigarettes were distributed, one to a patient, at ten in the
morning and two in the afternoon, at the large nurses' station
down where the corridors branched. In that vicinity, as the
hours for distribution approached, there was always a traffic
jam of wheelchairs, accompanied not infrequently by shoving
and displays of ill temper. As each "inmate" received his precious dole, he made for the TV Room, which was soon filled
with a choking blue haze. Sometimes a nurse or other person
passing through propped open the outside door that led to air
and sunlight; but the occupants seemed happier when it was
closed. Lura especially, whose face had a pasty, prison pallor,
became restless when the door was open. Only when I was
about to leave did I discover why.

Theoretically, each patient had a shower twice a week.
I believe the "shower mornings" for our room were Tuesday
and Saturday. But if we got one shower a week we could consider ourselves lucky. The institution was always shorthanded,

perennially on some sort of emergency schedule. The patient to be showered was wrapped in a sheet, placed on a commode/bathchair (hopefully the Cadillac), and wheeled through the corridors to the nearest empty shower room. At first I found it embarrassing to travel outside the privacy of my room with my bare bottom hanging out, but I soon realized that this was the universal experience. The shower stall had a waist-high wall on one side over which the attendant leaned in a sometimes fruitless attempt to protect her shoes and uniform. The patient was soaped, then rinsed; then the water was turned off and the commode pulled a little way out of the stall while the aide reached underneath and scrubbed the more personal parts. Then back, wrapped in the sheet, to be dressed for the day.

After Florence and I were dressed and the dauntless Lura had dressed herself and had her morning smoke, Florence sat in her electrically operated chair and slowly read her prayers, and I read whatever I could find to read (as time went on, I received some mail from Chemehuevi Valley, including magazines and an occasional book from one of my book clubs—but I was always short of reading material, gratefully borrowing gothic novels and even Reader's Digest Condensed Books from nurses' aides who had literary inclinations—I particularly remember Becky—and from the social workers). Lura always went unhesitatingly to the place where cigarettes were distributed; but on the way back from the TV Room she sometimes forgot her room number and had to appeal to passersby, "Which room am I in?" Back in 36, she looked first in her closet to see if something had been stolen during her absence, also to assure herself that she was in the right place; then she took her purse from her nightstand and sorted through its contents, and made comments on "the little old man sitting out in the sun."

This "little old man" was purely a product of imagination and defective vision, but Lura believed in him implicitly and wrathfully resisted any attempt to argue him away. The three or four houses facing on the dead-end street which we could see from our window all had air conditioners on their roofs. The corner house was large, probably a duplex, and its air conditioner was protected by an A-shaped roof. This, Lura insisted, was a little house with a porch on which an old man sat constantly taking the sun, or even "right out in the rain" during an occasional shower. The house itself was modern, built in a style suitable to the desert, with small windows high up under the eaves on the sunny side. Lura would not listen to me when I said that this was an architectural style, that the rooms were air-conditioned and adequately lighted. She vividly pictured a dark and airless interior, peopled either by criminals or the insane. The small, high windows were designed so that the inmates could not escape. And "the little old man sitting out on his porch" was alternately the prison guard or the keeper of the "loonies."

Florence said Lura was so insistent and so adamant that she had convinced the former occupant of the middle bed that such was indeed the truth and had even persuaded her that she too could see "the little old man." I soon learned to attempt no rebuttal. Any contradiction only evoked an almost terrifying flash of anger. This corner house fronted on the street that ran at right angles to us, and we seldom saw the inhabitants go in or out—in fact, I rather think they may have been away on vacation, for weeks elapsed before I saw anyone at all, and then there was a great airing of bedding and other activities that might attend the reopening of a house. But these things, when they came, went unnoticed by Lura, so firmly was her mind occupied with the image of inmates immured in hot, airless darkness.

Lura also frequently, almost daily, discussed her age, which as she gave it fluctuated between eighty-two, eighty-five, and eighty-seven. Once she confessed to bewilderment in this area. Unwisely, I offered, "Tell me what year you were born in, and we'll figure it out."

"I'm an old lady," Lura flared. "I can't be expected to remember stuff like that."

After that I usually talked to Florence or kept quiet. I never tired of being able to see out-of-doors. Outside the wall of the institution ran a ditch fringed with weeds. I knew it was a ditch because, when a pair of big dogs were taken for a run along the road, they sometimes tugged at their leashes and vanished into it. Beyond the ditch, the roadway. I do not remember it as paved, but if pavement there was, it had soft shoulders of golden brown dust. Beyond the road, the houses—three, I think, besides the large gray building that was the center of Lura's daytime fantasies—and back of the houses, trees, luxuriant and green, bordering the irrigation canal. The road or street was, as I've said, a dead-end and the traffic on it sparse: cars belonging to or visiting the homes that fronted it, an occasional bright yellow piece of road equipment. It was a good place to run dogs or canter horses, or for young people to jog in the clear morning light before the worst of the heat or late in the golden afternoons. Welcome reminders that there was a world not peopled by the helpless old and their attendants.

When the noon trays came, if I had not been ordered to the dining room, I ate with the wary smugness of a cat who, this once at least, has eluded the hand that would put her out. Sundays there was usually chicken, roasted I believe, one of the few dishes prepared with care, and actually palatable. And one Friday we had a salmon loaf, also appetizing. There were always the watery, funky-tasting mashed potatoes, and often the cheapest sort of canned mixed vegetables. When these were in a dubious cream sauce, Florence ate them. She was reminded of the rich and delicious sauces her mother used to put over vegetables. Her mother was French, and had been a marvelous cook. Twice there was cauliflower, overcooked to a grayish mash, but welcome to me, because it had started out fresh; and once there was overcooked cabbage. Florence couldn't eat vegetables of the cabbage family; so she was served instead with canned green beans until she tired of them, grew mildly petulant, and left them uneaten on her plate. The meat dish most often served and most loathsome was a flat patty of some substance that I believe was palmed

off as breaded veal. It tasted like no part of any animal I was
acquainted with, and contained tiny fragments of bone and
gristle. I was told by someone after I had been there several
weeks that it was made of ground beef and pork mixed with
some sort of vegetable protein; this was a product especially
manufactured for nursing homes, prisons, and similar institutions—or at least, so I was given to understand.

Soon after noonday dinner, Mike would put in an appearance. I tried to read, or after I had managed to get writing
materials, to write letters; anything not to intrude on the privacy that was no privacy. After the long years in big, two-
storied midwestern homes, after the intimacies and blendings
of more than fifty years, a husband and wife were reduced to
visits in a room with two other women! They were patient
and gracious; they made an effort now and then to include
me in their conversations. I was grateful. Also I was overcome
with embarrassment, overcome with shame that I could not
take myself off to a private place of my own. I too had the
memory of shared intimacy, long ago and far away.

Sometimes Mike took Florence out of the room in her
wheelchair, sometimes he walked with her. She walked very
well, stirring me to envy. If she could only get up by herself!
Every bit of strength gained brought "going home" that much
nearer. But no. Unless she could lift herself into the automatic
chair she couldn't make it. She was so fragile, her bones were
so fragile, so brittle. Once (before she came to Golden Mesa)
a nurse was helping her up from bed; and somehow there was
a twisting to one side, and a snap that was a bone snapping,
and the prelude to a return to St. Luke's Hospital and more
dreary months in a cast while it mended.

Lura secured her afternoon cigarette and went to the TV
Room to smoke it. That was invariable. Sometimes the afternoon brought Florence other visitors; usually other patients
or their visiting relatives. Once an elderly priest came, Father
Murphy, a man no longer active in his parish. He looked to be
as frail as Florence, and not quite of this world. Quite proper-

ly, he talked to Mike and Florence only. What would he have had to say to me or I to him? By background and belief (or nonbelief) I was excluded from that flock; and felt momentarily forlorn at this exclusion.

Morning or afternoon, at no particular time of day, just when she got around to it, the therapist, Dorothy Williams, came to walk with us by turns; or if I was still in bed, briefly to exercise my legs. But this was Mondays through Fridays only. Saturdays and Sundays, lacking a friend or relative to help me, I had no opportunity to walk, unless one of the aides was indulgent enough to allow me to make the brief journey from chair or bed to bathroom. At first I borrowed Florence's walker, later Dorothy brought me one which another patient no longer used.

At three-thirty there was a change of shift. We would listen for the approach of the "girls" to help us into bed. (In the morning, they worked singly; in the afternoon, in pairs.) With luck, they would be there between three-thirty and four-thirty. There would follow the welcome trip to the bathroom, a change into nightgown, and the blessed relief of stretching out in bed. But soon the beds were cranked up, the bed tables wheeled in place, and the carts approached with supper. Unless my bed was cranked high, I could not reach my food, but if left too long in this position, I suffered frightful cramps in my legs.

The evening meal was light: Invariably Sunday evening supper was cottage cheese and canned fruit, with a minute carton of watery ice cream or sherbet. Not bad, but monotonous. Sometimes we had something that was ostensibly macaroni and cheese (the cheese was imperceptible), served with a vegetable—usually canned zucchini in tomato sauce (and this in a land where every variety of squash and numerous other fresh vegetables glutted the market!). The absolute dietary low was reached the evening when we were served a "soup" consisting of the water in which wieners had been boiled, slightly thickened, with leftover canned stringed beans, a few pieces of leftover potatoes, and few thin slices of the basic wieners.

After supper I could watch the deepening golden glow of sunset. Rarely, when there were clouds, slashes of flame and crimson faded to pink and then to mauve, and ultimately gray as light ebbed from the sky. Beyond the trees, the greenish globes of streetlights appeared. (Lura insisted that each globe had "a little tail" through which the electricity ascended.) Floodlights went on outside the building. Then the "girls" came to draw the curtains and give us our final bedtime care—a bedpan, a brief back rub (sometimes), and for me an opportunity to get my dentures brushed, a service which Florence's husband had already performed for her.

Florence asked for her rosary and had her curtains drawn. I pulled on the light at the head of my bed and settled down to read. Sometimes Lura read too for a little while—usually aloud in a halting monotone. She read religious tracts, interspersed with fervent affirmations of belief, or accounts of tragedies in outdated *Reader's Digests*, accompanied by appropriate ejaculations of horror. Soon she pulled off her light. "I've got good eyes, I'm not going to ruin 'em. Look at her"—meaning me—"reading in that light! She don't care nothin' about her eyes! *I* wouldn't do that!" These acid comments kept up for a long time. If I endeavored to draw my curtain part way, the situation was only exacerbated. Lura seldom addressed anyone directly, and never spoke of anyone by name—always "he" or "she." I doubt if she knew names from one moment to the next. Sometimes if the evening "girls" crossed her, she reviled them and threatened to leave the Nursing Home.

"I'll have my sister come get me in the morning," she would announce grandly. "I wouldn't stay in a place like this."

Fifteen minutes later she would be insisting that the same "girl" who had aroused her indignation kiss her good night.

Or again, she might announce with pathetic bewilderment, "I was going home, but it got so late. I'm tired. I think I'll stay here overnight."

To which the attendant usually responded soothingly, "You are at home. This is your home." (That statement, meant to reassure, always struck through me like a blast from the deepest pit. What if the time should come when that would be as true for me as for Lura? What if that time had already come?)

Time, for Lura, was without a future tense. It consisted only of the immediate present, the present of the moment, and the remote past; and more often than not, especially in the small hours of the night, the past *was* the present, and there was no line of demarcation.

After the starched and authoritative RN's (Registered Nurses) in their stiff, lordly caps, or sometimes the equally starched and decidedly less authoritarian LVN's (Licensed Vocational Nurses) in less impressive caps, had given the final medication of the day; after Lura had received and grumblingly eaten her late snack; after the external sounds had dropped a few decibels as the inhabitants of the East Wing fell into their first sleep; when I had put my light out and the tiny, involuntary sounds of pain no longer came from Florence's bed—then Lura entered into her own.

Having extracted herself with uncanny agility from the restraint which was sometimes put on her at bedtime, she sat bolt upright in her flat bed, not leaning against the pillow which she had propped up on her headboard, rocking herself to and fro and talking in a deep monotone. She must have slept occasionally, nodding upright or leaning back against the pillow. (Sometimes one of the night attendants or a nurses' aide who happened to come in exclaimed, "You can't sleep that way!", put her pillow down flat, settled her on it, and tucked her in; and two minutes later Lura would be sitting up rocking back and forth.)

Our beds were separated only by the width of her nightstand. My hearing is acute, there was no way to shut out that rasping, unpleasant voice, and I had not enough self-control to sleep through it. I twisted, groaned, coughed, tried lying perfectly still in the hope my roommate would fall asleep. The soliloquy might start with repetitions of daytime maunderings about the prisoners or nuts shut up in the house across the road and "the little old man" who lived on the roof. Then as the boundaries between sleep and waking blurred, doors opened into deep and secret memories, and I listened, enthralled in spite of myself. . . .

> First I married Hal H-A-L, Hal W-I-L-L-S, Wills. Hal was a good man. He died. We had a little boy. His name was Jimmy. Jimmy was a good boy. I wonder what became of Jimmy? He must be a big boy now, he must be a grown man. Jimmy was always a good boy. He had to go to that home. . . .
> Then I married Hoffman. He was all right—I guess. I wonder whatever became of Hoffman? He was a Jew. Did he die? . . . Or did I divorce him?

Then thought might revert to Jimmy, or back to Jimmy's father. And just once or twice the voice changed, became welcoming, sweet, intimate: "Come in, darlin'. Ah-h-h, come in." Then I would try to close my ears, for there are moments which ought never to be shared with strangers. Then the hoarse, tired old voice would stop and there would be a few minutes of blessed silence. . . .

Lura never came back from her excursions for cigarettes without looking into her closet, as I have mentioned, to see which of her dresses had been stolen during her absence. Her only wrap was a bright green terry-cloth robe, and once one of the attendants hung a sweater in her closet and tried to put it on her. This intrusion was resented. Additions to her wardrobe were resented as much as real or imaginary losses—the only real loss occurred when an aide threw her odorous slip in the laundry hamper and the laundry mislaid it. Her only footgear was a pair of bright pink cloth slippers. Almost daily she remembered that she had had shoes, and declared that her sister had stolen them. (But Florence remembered that in a moment of rationality Lura had given them willingly to her sister, because she had no use for them.) Almost daily the coarse-toothed black comb would be declared stolen until an exasperated "girl" dumped out the pack rat's nest that filled her purse and located it, together with an ashtray or two to be returned to the TV Room.

And sometimes the delusion of present loss entered into the night fantasies:

> I used to walk with a cane. It was a good, black cane. Pa sneaked in here one night and took it. He's got no use for it—jes' took it out of meanness. Pa always was selfish—never gave us kids a thing. Ma had to support the family. She took in washing and wove rag carpets. . . .

As I listened a vision came into my mind, bright and clear. Was there a telepathic transferral of Lura's thought? Or did the words call up composite memories from my Texas childhood? Perhaps my own weakness made me peculiarly susceptible to the fantasies of a disintegrating mind. Or perhaps the words "rag carpets" triggered a deeply buried memory of my mother driving out in the buggy to take her own carefully spliced strips of cloth wound into balls to some poor woman on the outskirts of town who took in washing and wove rag rugs for a living. Whatever the explanation, what I experienced had almost the sharpness of hallucination. I mentally saw an unkempt yard enclosed by a neglected picket fence with a sagging gate; scraggly trees from whose limbs hung one or two rope swings; and a great black steaming pot propped up on bricks over an outdoor fire. I smelled woodsmoke and boiling soapy water—hot soapsuds made with strong yellow homemade lye soap. At the same time I saw beyond the porch with the loose boards into the bare room where stood a primitive loom flanked by stacked up balls of rags prepared for weaving. . . .

My nights passed between longing for the oblivion of sleep and an unwilling fascination with Lura's monologues. Towards morning she would quiet down and I would fall asleep, only to be awakened around four o'clock by the cries of a blind, senile woman two doors down on the opposite side of the corridor. If she was reasonably comfortable, she sang Silent Night over and over, off-key, in an old cracked voice; if she was suffering, she ceaselessly cried, "Help me! Somebody help me!" or uttered wordless ululations.

Nights were in one respect more tolerable than days: The night "girls" usually came with reasonable promptness when I put on my light and were not reluctant to assist with the bedpan. Therefore I felt free to drink all the water I wanted from the plastic pitcher on my bedside tray. (Sometimes they were slower removing the bedpan than bringing it; one night Florence was left unattended on her bedpan for forty minutes.)

3

By day Lura not infrequently regaled us with accounts of
her days as a dancing teacher ("tap and toe dancing"), and
the darling little girls who had made up her classes. She had
pink satin slippers "at home" to prove she had taught toe
dancing. Florence cautiously wondered if this wasn't another
of her daydreams. But when the Maricopa County doctor
who came to see her at intervals asked her to show him what
action she had in her "good" leg, I had proof of her veracity
in this matter. Lura flung her leg skyward in an unmistakable
gesture—and I saw that her toes were permanently molded into the shape of a ballet shoe.

This doctor was a tall gray man with a wryly humorous
face. He looked like an old-fashioned general practitioner of
the better type. He overheard me complaining that I had not
had my blood pressure checked since arriving at Golden Mesa.
Later, passing me in the corridor, he remarked, "I can take
your blood pressure. But I won't tell you what it is." I wanted
to retort, "Ah! The mystique of the medicine man!" But discretion prevailed.

There was another County doctor, a brisk, blond young
man, who came to see Lura. Also there was a young woman

77

psychologist or psychiatrist, who sat beside Lura every few weeks and went through a list of questions.

Pencil in hand, checking off replies, she asked, "Do you know what year this is? What month? What day of the week?"

Lura wouldn't attempt to answer. She was an old lady and couldn't be bothered.

"Do you know what city we're in?"

Momentarily Lura's face expressed a pathetic disorientation.

"Los Angeles, I guess," she said uncertainly.

The young woman looked shocked, presumably at this evidence of deterioration. "Why, this is Phoenix! Don't you remember that you're in Phoenix?"

I have said that Lura retained no memory of the present. But weeks or so later I had proof that she seemingly could remember if she put her will to it. When the young woman asked, "Do you know what city we are in?" Lura responded tartly, "Phoenix! Where did you think we were?"

Once a month, early in the morning, fasting, and over her strenuous objections, Lura was taken for examination to the County Hospital. This was evidently a traumatic experience— not the examination, which seemed to make little or no impression, but the journey itself. Returning, she once told Florence and me that she had been lost, alone in her wheelchair, downtown "in all that traffic." But somehow she had managed to wheel herself "home."

Florence said that sometime prior to my arrival, Lura had broken a leg. (I assume she had been ambulatory, although perhaps not too steady on her feet, up until that mishap.) She had stayed in the hospital for a time, then was sent back to the Nursing Home with her leg in splints. But no sooner was she left alone in her bed than she managed, with great strength and dexterity, to remove the splints. So she had had to be taken back to the hospital, and returned in a cast.

If the attention Lura received is typical, I must admit that County patients received good medical care. In fairness I must say this, however much I disapprove of the practice, legal in Arizona, of taking a charity patient's entire Social Security check. At least these patients were seen regularly by their doctors.

With the exception of the County physicians, the only doctor I saw during my entire stay was Florence's private physician, called in by her husband when she contracted a severe cold. I know there were other doctors on call, although there was no resident physician. A woman died just down the corridor from us one night, and I am sure she did not die without medical attention; but unless summoned by a member of the patient's family, it seemed that physicians appeared only in cases of extreme emergency.

Upon entering Golden Mesa, one was confronted by a conspicuous notice stating that patients would only be admitted after thorough examination by a physician. When I received no such examination, I assumed it was because of a report by Dr. Bertman. I came to believe that this was not the case, and that the rule about examinations was very laxly enforced. As soon as I was transferred from the gurney to a bed in The Ward, a plastic bracelet was put upon my wrist (beside the one I still wore from Indian Hospital) giving my name and the name of Dr. Hawke. I said, "I don't know any Dr. Hawke," and was told, "He's your doctor; he'll see you later."

Dr. Hawke never saw me. When the supplies of Darvocet, Benadryl, and Vitamin C which I had brought from Indian Hospital ran out, he issued prescriptions. (He also prescribed aspirin, as I discovered when, on departure, I was handed a container with—I think—fifty tablets. My records plainly stated that I was allergic to aspirin. I assume it was a run-of-the-mill prescription for each new arrival.) Sleepless nights were wearing me down, so I asked for a sleeping tablet. Dr. Hawke prescribed large, oval, dark green capsules. I was of course not told the name. Instructions said, "Take two at bedtime," but various night nurses advised me to "get by on one" if I could, and after I voluntarily reduced myself to one,

refused to give me a second. Only on leaving did I discover
that the drug was Chloral Hydrate, and that two capsules
probably constituted a "Mickey Finn" strong enough to knock
out a mule.

I was concerned about my blood pressure and had other
problems I wished to discuss with a physician. I was told
soothingly, "Dr. Hawke usually comes in around the first of
the month." The first of October came and went, and there
was no Dr. Hawke. Early in November I was told that "Dr.
Hawke is in the hospital, but he is very busy." I said, "Yes,
Virginia, there is a Dr. Hawke!" The nurse looked at me in
a startled way which said: "Why, she is senile after all!" Her
name wasn't Virginia, and besides, we weren't supposed to
call nurses by their first names—only the "girls" were so
addressed.

RN's were very exalted beings. They bustled about in their
starched caps and immaculate uniforms, bearing trays of
medication, morning, noon, and night. If you needed something in between, you told your nurses' aide (if she saw fit to
answer your light), and she said, "I'll see if there is a nurse in
this wing." If there was no one at the nurses' station or making rounds, you were out of luck. Registered nurses did not
take temperatures or blood pressures, and temperature and
blood-pressure checks were not part of the daily routine. If
need arose, a "girl" was called from whatever she might be
doing to perform the needed chore. This was cause for grum-
bling among the aides. Once a "girl" was called to take a blood
pressure when she was in the midst of getting me up for the
day. She had to leave me damp, naked, and sitting on the
commode.

Some of the RN's were more congenial than others. There
were one or two with whom I felt at ease, but now even their
names are gone from my memory. But I distinctly remember
one who was our evening nurse for a good part of my stay. She
was a competent and conscientious professional. When, some
months before my arrival, Florence contracted pneumonia,

this nurse had been alert enough to see that she had prompt medical attention. But she was also dictatorial and capable of petty tyranny, and neither Florence nor I found her congenial. Most of the nurses walked with a light tread; this woman's feet came down heavily: thump, thump, thump. Her mouth was tightly closed, cutting a straight, thin, unsmiling line across her face. To myself, I called her the Dragon Lady, and was indiscreet enough to refer to her in that way before one of the aides. I realized my slip, and swore her to silence; but the appellation spread like wildfire.

The Dragon Lady and I were engaged in a running feud, a perpetual contest of wills. For a time she reached our room very early in her evening rounds, usually prior to 7:30 p.m. She insisted that I take my sleeping pill at that time. Since we had not yet had our final bedpans and back rubs, and since the noise level was still high in the corridors, I felt it was far too early to try to sleep. The few times that I obediently took the medication at that time, I inevitably fought off its effects and the result was an excess of nervous tension, a high which prevented my getting any sleep or even restful relaxation. I suggested, it seemed to me quite sensibly, that she leave the capsule for me to take later in the evening. This of course was absolutely contrary to ethical nursing practice. I then suggested that she stop by later, just prior to leaving the East Wing, and give the medication then. This she refused to do—quite justifiably, perhaps, from her standpoint. In a place of that size no nurse could be expected to give medication at the whim of the patient. The Dragon Lady said I could take my capsule in her presence, when it was convenient for her to give it to me, or not at all. I tried refusing it and requesting it about midnight, after the shift changed. But sometimes our attendant couldn't locate the nurse on duty, and even when she was contacted, there was a great hassle, arguments on my part, and records to be consulted on hers, since it was not her duty to give medication at that hour. Finally the Dragon Lady began to come by a little later. I professed myself ready to go to sleep, complained about the size of the "horse pill," and made a great production of pretending to swallow it, while secreting it in my cheek. When she had turned away or left the room, I removed it and took it later, when I was really ready for sleep. I suspected that no one was fooled, but authority was preserved and I had my way.

LVN's (Licensed Vocational Nurses) ranked considerably below RN's. Their caps seemed softer and lower than the high, stiffly starched caps worn by RN's at Golden Mesa, they were generally younger, more approachable, and a little less sure of themselves. They did not as a rule administer medication, although I seem to recall times when no RN was on duty and the medicine tray was brought around by an LVN. Occasionally, in case of emergency, certain LVN's were not above giving or removing a bedpan.

The most important persons in our lives, the real arbiters of our daily destinies, were the nurses' aides, the "girls." I could not hazard a guess as to how many "girls" worked in Golden Mesa. I believe the number fluctuated, for in addition to those permanently established in Phoenix and helping to support families, there were others more or less impermanent, who worked for a while and quit or were fired. But there were never quite enough to keep the place running smoothly, and I am sure the constant shifting from wing to wing and from one group of patients to another did not improve efficiency. Nevertheless, some of the "girls" were very efficient, especially those who had trained elsewhere. Arizona, however, being a "right to work" state, the wage of $1.95 an hour (the same paid to housekeepers) was not calculated to attract employees whose experience and training would qualify them for higher pay. (An Indian girl who had trained in the large Indian Hospital in Phoenix said that as a U.S. Government employee she had received $2.50 an hour.)

Gussie was frequently assigned to Room 36. She was a black woman, handsome in a sculptured sort of way, extremely tall—over six feet, I think (she said she had a son attending the University of Arizona who was six feet four)—and with the most erect, haughty carriage I ever saw on anyone.

I called her the African Queen, but not, you may be sure, to her face. As a rule she treated Florence and me with courtesy stretched like a thin veneer over contempt. Sometimes the contempt broke through, as on the morning when Florence had been quite exacting about precisely which nightgown/slip she wanted with which dress and I had insisted on having my call button placed where I could reach it from my wheelchair (which did not guarantee that it would be answered). On this occasion Gussie said, "You two think you're the only patients in this place." I think we both turned a little pale. There is no denying that we were afraid of Gussie. Usually she did her work quickly and efficiently, sometimes unbent to converse briefly, and took particular pains with Florence's lovely hair, because she liked doing hair and had considerable skill as a hairdresser. Lura she ignored, except for handing her her slip and dress. I believe she was the one who located Lura's slip, or one she could use, after it had been lost in the laundry; and on another occasion when Lura insisted her slip had been lost, Gussie drew it out from under her pillow and handed it to her with wordless disdain. Gussie was the girl who most openly expressed resentment when called from her regular duties to take a temperature.

Callie was a black woman of uncertain age, possibly older than Jewell, though she didn't look it. She had a very nice home, and eight Siamese cats, had taken a trip to Hawaii the previous year and was planning another tour of some sort. It was hard to see how she could manage all this on $1.95 an hour, although she collected meat scraps from dinner trays to feed her cats. I overheard a remark, typical of racial attitudes in Phoenix, in which a visitor expressed wonder that "her sort" should consider traveling. I later learned that she was working two shifts, one at Golden Mesa and one at another Phoenix nursing home, and getting by most nights with three hours sleep. This was enough to account for her brusque and unsocial manner. I had thought that our common interest in cats might be a point of contact, but she did not respond to my overtures. One morning an announcement came over the public address system that since the Home was shorthanded, the "girls" might use their discretion as to which patients to get up for the day. Callie approached my bed with a basin of soapy water. "What's that for?" I asked suspiciously.

"I'm going to give you a bed bath. I've got fourteen rooms and I don't have time to get you up."

"I want to go to the toilet."

"You can use the bedpan."

As I began to try to sit up, Callie took my arm and said, "I'm your nurse. I know what's best for you."

I have a congenital dread of conflict, a timidity then enhanced by a sense of helplessness. But the dreadful vision of myself as a chronic bedpatient armed me with the courage of desperation. I grasped Callie's arm as firmly as she had grasped mine. "I am not a bedpatient," I said without a tremor, "and I am here for therapy, not to be turned into one. Give me the walker."

Callie got me up. There was a sort of armed truce between us until an incident occurred which put her in my power. I was sitting on the commode. Callie had filled the washbasin with soapy water and told me to wash myself. Then she left me to go on some unknown errand. My short, arthritic arms could not reach into the basin. Feeling stronger than usual, I thought I would maneuver myself over till I could get a firm grip on the edge, pull myself up, and stand braced against the washstand. But I had overestimated my ability. The washbasin was slippery, my grasp uncertain, and when I tried to stand, I couldn't hold on and the commode slid out from under me. I ended up on the floor. When Callie opened the bathroom door and saw me, her expression was beyond words to describe. A patient had fallen while she was supposedly in attendance. Worse yet, an alert and articulate patient who could make complaints, demand X-rays, bring suit if some fragile old bone had happened to crack. She must have seen herself not only losing her job, but blacklisted and without any work at all.

I have had many falls and this was by no means the most serious. I knew I wasn't hurt.

I said, "Callie, if you can manage to get me up without calling for help, I swear that I will never say a word to anyone about this."

She still looked dazed, and I said, "I'm all right. I fall easy, like a cat." And then I added, "If you are strong enough to pull me up, we'll say nothing about it to anyone."

Callie developed what appeared to be superhuman strength. She pulled me to my feet, almost, it seemed, without effort, and eased me back onto the commode. Nothing was said about my weight or a possibly strained back. The sketchy toilet was completed, and I walked a few steps with the walker out to my wheelchair. The episode was never again mentioned between us. I never tried to blackmail Callie in any way; but neither did she ever again cross me in my reasonable requests. And I kept my word, and did not speak of the fall— I think not even to Florence.

There were fewer complaints about my weight here than in Indian Hospital. However, I continued to slip down towards the foot of the hospital bed and to need to be pulled back up by the evening "girls" when they made their final visit. They made a production of it, taking hold of me, sometimes quite painfully, one on each side. But one aide, young, pretty, and not very strong looking, had a better system. She reached over the head of the bed, grasped me under both arms, and pulled me up in one quick, smooth motion. I thought that I would never forget her, but now her name has slipped from memory. She was paired with Dicey, the only black girl besides Hattie to work the evening shift; and she always waited to put me in position until Dicey had left the room for a moment. It seems that the Head Nurse had ruled that two "girls" must always work together to pull a patient up in bed; she did not want them straining their backs—although the other method was actually easier for anyone who had been trained to do it correctly. My friend was afraid that Dicey would tattle on her.

I didn't think Dicey would do such a thing. She impressed me as a very good person. She was remarkably patient with Lura, who would rail at her one moment and insist on being kissed good night the next. I had been given a subscription to a Unity Church publication, the *Daily Word*, and had one copy of that small magazine with me, tucked into my purse. Statements which might once have seemed to me saccharine and simplistic now gave me a small bit of comfort, and I read the thoughts for each day as faithfully as Florence read her prayers for the sick. Seeing it, Dicey remarked: "I read that too. You have to have something to hold on to."

The name Dicey impressed me. I had not heard it since I was a child visiting my aunt in southern Texas, where there were many "colored people." Dicey, Hattie, Callie were all old-fashioned names, anachronistic in the 1970's.

Becky was sometimes paired with Dicey. She was a pleasant, blond girl who wore spectacles and sympathized with my desire to read. She loaned me gothic novels from her large collection. They seemed to suit my mental capacity. I am eternally grateful to the *Daily Word* and the novels of Victoria Holt for giving me anchors to sanity that I was able to grasp. I am convinced that if the brain is functioning on a reduced supply of oxygen it requires a constant effort, an unremitting effort of the will, not to slip into that state of incoherent reverie which seems pleasant and natural. That was a line of least resistance that many of my fellow "inmates" seemed to have taken.

Mr. Dole's disjointed soliloquies were a prime example of that sort of thinking, thinking which was an absence of thought. Lura was drifting that way, although her fantasies still had a certain form and substance; and she proved that she could still drag herself back to a certain brief contact with reality when she really wished to do so. The end result of mental slippage was to be seen in a very aged woman who for some reason was "got up" each day, fastened into a wheelchair, and placed in the corridor near the door of our room. There she sat, presumably sightless, eyes closed, toothless, sucking on her knuckles like an infant with a pacifier. One day her whole forearm was covered with Band-Aids; I was told that "one of the 'girls' had taken hold of her"—roughly, I assume. Apparently the paper-thin skin of extreme age had rubbed off in her grasp.

The physical therapist, Dorothy Williams, was of tremendous assistance to me in holding onto hope and sanity. She never talked down to me, never addressed me as "honey" or "dearie"—which, on the lips of the nursing staff, sounded as insincere as the endearments of prostitutes. When I asked her opinion about the possibility of a hip operation, she was careful to remind me that she was not a physician. But, she said cautiously, at my age she personally would be reluctant to undergo that operation. There was the risk of prolonged anesthesia, and the surgery itself would be a profound shock to the body. Besides, she added, she thought I "could cope very well without surgery."*

When Dorothy took me to practice walking with the aid of the walker, she held my left arm lightly, less to steady me than to enable her to become instantly aware of any faltering on my part, and with her left hand she drew the wheelchair along behind us. Long experience had made her very adept at performing this somewhat awkward maneuver. She was ready in an instant to let the wheelchair go and support her patient with both arms if the need arose.

At first we went no farther than the door of Room 36. Later I was able to go to the top of the little ramp, and sometimes, to practice turning, into the TV Room. One memorable day I walked down the ramp (a rather scary undertaking) and almost to the large nurses' station where cigarettes were given out. And occasionally we walked in the other direction, all

*Eventually I disregarded her advice. In 1975 I had total and successful hip surgery, which relieved me of the constant pain I had suffered for so many years—although, because of a curvature of the spine, it did not enable me to walk much better. But I remain eternally grateful to Dorothy for the thoughtful attention she gave to my problem, and to me as a human being.

the way to the tightly closed outside door at the end of the corridor that ran the length of the East Wing. However, I was never allowed to try to walk back. Dorothy always feared I might get too tired or too unsteady and pushed me back in the wheelchair. Often I moaned, "If I could only walk two hundred yards at a time!" My kind helper always answered reassuringly, "You will. You will."

Once, passing Lura sitting in the wheelchair beside her bed, I exclaimed, "I wish I was as strong-willed as that one!" This was on one of those days when I had lost out in my constant struggle not to go to the dining room, while Lura, as usual, had eaten where she pleased. Dorothy looked at me in amazement. "What makes you think you're not?" she asked. Lura, it seemed, would not make any consistent effort to walk with a walker and was even reluctant to exercise on the bars in the Therapy Room. Having attained mastery of her wheelchair, she had come to prefer that less laborious way of getting about. This to me evidenced her strong if perverted will; but Dorothy must have classified it as simple laziness.

Once only during the period when I worked with Dorothy I suffered a sudden attack of the loss of coordination which had caused me such embarrassment at Indian Hospital and has, at lessening intervals, continued to plague me since. We happened to be in the TV Room at the time. Dorothy managed to ease me into a chair, then got me back into the wheelchair. She said, "I was frightened. It seemed like you were fainting." I replied, "My body fainted, not my mind."

Dorothy was a massive woman, very sturdy, and during the hours she spent on duty, I do not believe she rested for a moment. Sometimes she came to the dining room and "took" a patient who was seated at the table waiting for her tray, overruling protests with the blunt statement, "If I don't take you now, I can't take you at all." She wore sensible clothes, loose-fitting jumpers in solid colors over white blouses. I do not remember her face distinctly, merely that it was kind and strong. But I will never forget her strong, tireless legs, her supporting arms, and her equally supportive mental attitude.

The air conditioning in Golden Mesa was eccentric. Going along the corridor, one passed through zones of heat and zones of chill. Room 36 was almost always cooler than I found comfortable in the daytime. Dorothy Williams gave me a sweater, pale blue and hand knit. She said more sweaters had been given her (possibly by grateful patients) than she would ever use.

Paired with Dorothy Williams in my mind is Ann Keim, the social worker; a woman of uncertain age, with hair colored a striking red and an apparently inexhaustible wardrobe of smart clothes. She was my link with the outside world and my friends. With money I had on deposit in the office, she bought me two crisp flowered dusters and slips to go with them. (I had suggested panties, but such refinements as panties and bras were for patients who could dress themselves.) She also took my checks to cash, bought me a writing tablet, envelopes and stamps. She delivered letters to me, when they began to arrive, and sometimes took my letters to mail—though I usually gave them to Mr. Kramer.

I was now writing letters to everyone whose address I could remember. Harry Lawton, Chairman of the Editorial Board of Malki Museum Press, and Anne Jennings, my very dear friend and the first person with the Press to recognize my writing ability, were not among them. For over two months they did not know my whereabouts, and I still don't know precisely how I was "found." But I do know that during this time ever so gradually I began to doubt my own identity. Ever so tentatively, usually in the dead of night, a suggestion came to me: Do I really have two books in press? Do I really have prospects of some sort, however modest? Or am I entertaining a delusion, like so many of my fellow "inmates"? I had seen enough of them to recognize as delusion their mention of a son, or daughter, or other relative (if the patient was very old, very senile, it was "my mother") who was about to take the speaker "home," or perhaps it was a sister, who "has a good job waiting for me." I had always wanted to write, tried to cultivate the art of writing. Now perhaps, in age and

helplessness, I was imagining success. I firmly repudiated this
suggestion; but it did not go away, it hovered in dark recesses,
patiently awaiting its time. . . . (Could I deny, something
sinister whispered, that I *had* suffered a delusion my first
night in Indian Hospital?) That was why I was so grateful
when Ann Keim said, "Mail call!" and handed me a card or
letter from someone who at least knew my name.

Crystal, the social director (I was never quite sure of her
last name), completed the triumvirate of middle-aged women
outside the nursing staff who guided our destinies. She organ-
ized various divertissements, some of them useful and even
pleasant, others—considering the mental and physical condition of the somtimes unwilling participants—positively maca-
bre. (All of these entertainments were useful to the institution; they buttressed the claim that "patients in Golden Mesa
are kept active.") Crystal, too, was a large woman, beautifully
dressed. She always approached me courteously, urging me
to take part in whatever activity was afoot; I most often refused—frequently churlishly, I'm sorry to say.

The Hobby Room, supervised by Crystal, provided good
therapy for many patients. Florence was inordinately proud
of her achievement in producing two small plaques by cutting out various figures from magazine advertisements and
pasting them on wood (I think) to form a composite picture,
then varnishing the finished product. It was marvelous that
she could even hold scissors in her poor, misshapen hands,
and it must have been a painful process. But she said happily
that she had had "only a little help with the tail" (of a mouse
or some other small creature). From the Hobby Room also
emanated those bright posters, first witches, black cats, and
pumpkins to herald Halloween, and later more pumpkins
(not cut out), sheafs of grain, and the like, foretelling Thanksgiving. (These posters, like all the permanent pictures, were
predominately in tones of yellow and orange, carrying out
the theme of "the Golden Years." I used to long to see a picture of spring flowers, or a tropical forest, or a mother and

child—anything to get away from that continual suggestion of sunsets and Harvest Homes.)

I never visited the Hobby Room, but I did go with Florence a couple of times to play Bingo. Once I believe Mike pushed me and another time Crystal herself took me, and arranged for someone to wheel me back. The games were held in the dining room, which doubled as recreation room, and I could have wheeled myself, but once a day was all my arms could take. When we were seated someone said, "She's new, you help her." The answer was, "She doesn't need help." Many players required constant supervision, and all cards were inspected after each game to see that there were no errors and no false claims. Prizes were small cellophane bags of hard candy. I gave mine to one of the housekeepers who frequently mentioned her children, and I think Florence did the same.

Birthday parties, a collective one each month for everyone born in that month, were held in the dining room, and I found them worth attending. A passable fruit punch was served (Hawaiian Punch, or something of that sort) with plenty of chipped ice, and there were little squares of freshly baked cake. Guests of honor sat at the head table in the middle of the room, and women honorees had corsages. Sometimes there were gifts, I suppose from absent family or friends. There was a generally festive air, which Crystal worked hard to maintain, and patients on the whole were on their good behavior. Now and then someone, most often an old man, proved recalcitrant: He either didn't want to sit at the head table, or wanted to sit there when he wasn't one of the birthday people. The latter instances were harder to handle, since sometimes the ones who were entitled to honor didn't want someone else horning in. When disputes were settled and everyone served, Crystal and Ann Keim, with great vigor and an assumed jollity, led the cracked old voices in singing, "Happy birthday to you!"

Mrs. Mercer, the manager, did not attend these parties, though she was sometimes in evidence at more pretentious affairs. She was a superior being and the supreme ruler of this little kingdom. When I first saw her, looking up from my wheelchair, she was wearing a pleated brown skirt, somewhat shorter than a miniskirt, flaring out above long, knobby brown legs, and nipped in at the waist with a broad leather belt. Above it she wore a sleeveless green blouse from which extended long, knobby brown arms. Above the blouse was a thin, sharp-featured face. She had the sort of dry, brown skin that Caucasians of the athletic type acquire in the desert—that is, unless they happen to be florid. I immediately (and silently) dubbed her the Grasshopper Lady, but in this case I had sense enough to keep the wretched little witticism to myself. I didn't even tell Florence. Speaking kindly of everyone, she said she thought Mrs. Mercer "very nice," and that once she had been "very kind" to Mike and Jeanette, inviting them to use the phone in her office when some family emergency arose; but both Florence and her husband were heard to wonder "why Mrs. Mercer wore such *short* skirts."

In this catalogue of women important in our lives, I have almost forgotten to mention the dietician. I only saw her once during my whole stay at Golden Mesa. She came briskly into our room one morning to interview Florence and me about our reaction to the food we were being served. She said she tried to keep the meals well balanced and to please everyone, although of course we would understand that in an institution of that size, there could be no catering to individual tastes, everyone would have to eat the same things. We meekly agreed to everything. Both of us had been wanting an opportunity to voice our complaints, but when it was briefly offered, we totally failed to take advantage of it. We indicated that meals were satisfactory, and that we understood the problems involved—and afterwards wondered pointlessly why we had not spoken of any of our true feelings. I prefer to think that we were not so much craven as hypnotized by positive statements emanating from a strong personality.

These curious lapses, the failures of nerve and of purpose, that afflict those who are institutionalized, who feel themselves at the mercy of others . . . surely they make a bitter sense. The helpless one will bear the ills he has rather than court others that he knows not of.

There were only two regular male employees of whom we were aware (periodically a young orderly was hired to help the "girls" with the more difficult men patients, but not one of these stayed on the job long enough to be worth mentioning).

Joe Mushgrove was a Canadian by birth. A nurse employed at Golden Mesa had gone to Canada on her vacation, and met Joe and married him, and he had come back to Arizona with her. I suppose his official title was maintenance man. It might have been indispensable man. Early each morning he unlocked the closets where brooms, mops, and other pieces of equipment used by the housekeeping staff were kept. He tinkered tirelessly and patiently with the temperamental air conditioner, adjusting thermostats in an endeavor to satisfy the demands of patients who were always too warm as well as those who where always too cold. Joe was the man who installed and took out television sets and saw that they ran properly. (Black and white televisions could be rented for ten dollars per month, but I think the only color TV sets were privately owned.) He tried his best to keep worn-out wheelchairs serviceable, and he listened cheerfully to all complaints. And every day we looked out the window and saw Joe working in the grounds, watering, pruning, weeding. Even the most cantankerous patients agreed that he was a "nice man."

Abner was not a candidate for the "nice man" classification. He made no effort to please anyone, although he occasionally talked to patients who struck him as intelligent. I never knew his last name. He was a much older man than Joe; rumor said Abner was in his seventies. Rumor also had it that he was very well-to-do and just worked because he wanted to. He had charge over the linen: sheets, pillowcases, bedspreads, the adult-size cotton-flannel diapers, towels, and washclothes. The latter items were always in short supply, and many of the sheets were so thin that contact with an untrimmed toenail would rip them. The Home had recently acquired new bedspreads, pink for our end of the East Wing, blue in the smaller, two-bed rooms, and green in The Ward and the "Medicare Section." These dressed up the rooms very nicely, and made a favorable impression on visitors walking through. They also made the "girls" more adamant than ever about keeping patients out of bed in the daytime. Word had gone out that they were to be kept clean as long as possible without washing. Abner came in our room for something or other one day when I happened to be alone. "Look at this!" he exploded, holding up a crumpled, shrunken pink rag that looked as if it could never again be straightened out to cover a bed. "I told her [the Grasshopper Lady] to get something decent, I told her to get nylon! No, she had to get this cheap rayon! These things'll never be any good after they're washed. But no, all she can think about is saving a nickel."

Abner had sole control over the housekeeping women, including hiring and firing. They didn't like him. Deanna, the big, pretty black woman who was my favorite housekeeper, thought he was getting senile—"he don't remember nothin' " was the way she put it. She said he would fire a woman in the evening and call up the next morning to ask why she hadn't showed up for work. Once when she failed to catch her ride to work, he called up and ordered her to take a cab; but at her wages ($1.95 an hour, the same as the aides) she could spend pretty near all she earned in a day on a cab ride, and on top of that she would have to give the baby-sitter a little something. No sir, it wouldn't pay her to come to work if she had to hire a cab.

I knew Deanna's husband was out of work, and asked why he couldn't baby-sit for her. No, she said resignedly, "that 'ud be worse than no baby-sitter—if he'd do it, which for sure he wouldn't. He'd beat the oldest boy somethin' awful when he couldn't find his car keys, and all the time they were right there where he'd dropped them, on the ground by the car." Deanna was twenty-two, her husband eleven years older.

They'd been married when she was fifteen. He'd been out of work a long time now. Through her eyes, although she voiced few complaints, I saw a proud, embittered black man, working off his frustrations on whatever helpless thing he could lay his hands on. But Deanna had recently returned to the church, made her peace with God, and accepted the Lord Jesus Christ as her Saviour. Her eyes shown, her face lit up with newfound joy, her dimple flashed in and out. She was going to live a Christian life, and try not to be mean to anyone, not even her husband. And she had put her two little boys in Sunday School so they could grow up knowing Jesus.

Members of the housekeeping staff were strictly forbidden to touch the patients or to assist them in any way. But if no one was in sight who would snitch, Deanna would push my wheelchair up the ramp or sometimes along the corridor. There was a curious but profound rapport between us.

Deanna promised to bake me a sweet-potato pie for Thanksgiving. My concept of God is not precisely the same as hers; nonetheless I thank Him with all devoutness that I was not there to eat it!

Another housekeeper who impressed herself on my memory, although I never spoke to her beyond "Good morning" and have forgotten her name, was a white woman, almost as tall and big-boned as Deanna, though not nearly so heavy. She wasn't as pretty as Deanna, but she had a strikingly beautiful mane of tawny hair, falling down below her hips, and a pale skin that would have been beautiful if it had been free of blemishes. She and her smaller, less spectacular sister both held housekeeping jobs. The woman with the wonderful hair was married during my sojourn in Limbo. It was rumored that her young man had money, and that his folks were paying for the wedding. The entire staff of Golden Mesa was invited, black as well as white (which surprised and pleased me, in view of what I knew of racial attitudes current in Phoenix), and I believe that everyone went who wasn't actually on duty at the time or at the very least, everyone in the lower echelons. Dicey gave me details of the wedding. The bride had her hair piled high in a marvelous coiffure, and she (of course!) wore a beautiful white dress with veil. The wedding reception was elaborately catered, and there was a champagne fountain— or were there two champagne fountains? Also, of course, a popular music group. A Cinderella story, if ever there was one—and the beauty of it was that all the underpaid drudges were touched by the magic wand, for this one night at any rate.

One week later the unspectacular sister was unspectacularly married. Was it that her young man didn't have money, or couldn't the family endure two such splurges in succession? Or possibly this bride wanted something quieter. Anyway, the end result was that Golden Mesa was left shorthanded in the housekeeping department; but then they were perennially shorthanded in most departments.

Florence patronized the beauty parlor. One day, with some trepidation, I decided to have a permanent. Anne Keim applauded the idea and thought I should have my hair tinted, but I felt that would be a little extreme. On a certain Thursday afternoon, Leanne MacDonald (I'm guessing at her first name) came to wheel me down to the place set aside for beautification of the patients. It proved to be a small, shabby, cluttered room—and I now learned that Ann Keim's "office" was a cluttered desk in one corner! I was amazed; it seemed to me that anyone as busy as the social worker rated something much better.

Leanne was small, brisk, competent, and extremely adept at handling the aged. She had no sooner set to work on my sparse gray hair than Hilda, one of the ambulatory (extraordinarily ambulatory) denizens of the East Wing walked in and demanded a permanent. The operator said, "I'll put you down for next Thursday." Hilda, a big, domineering woman, said peremptorily, "Not next Thursday, now!" She plumped herself down in the chair where I would soon be sitting under the dryer. Leanne said, "I can't do it now, Hilda." Hilda said, "Son of a bitch! NOW!" I didn't know what would happen next—I myself happened to be afraid of Hilda. Leanne didn't seem disturbed. Shortly Crystal came in, sized up the situation and volunteered sotto voce, "I'll take her for a little walk and she'll forget all about it." She went up and said something to Hilda—I think she told her she urgently needed her advice on something—and they went out and returned no more while I was being beautified.

When the process was finished, I asked, "How much?" and Leanne said, "Twelve fifty." I said, "I don't want to deplete the little bit of cash I have in the office, I'll give you a check." She went out quickly, to find out, I presume, if I really had a bank account or merely the delusion of a bank account. When she came back, she told me how to spell her name and accepted the check without demur.

For two or three days I had a rather nice wave. Then Jewell came in and wielded a vigorous brush, and after that I had a frizz. I didn't mind. The light at the head of my bed was attached to a string which for some unknown reason terminated in a safety pin. After the light was turned on in the evening, I hooked the (closed) safety pin in my frizzy hair and had no difficulty locating the string when I wanted to turn the light off.

4

I had not been long in Room 36 when I became aware of hearing the voice of a child. Now children were seldom brought to Golden Mesa by visiting parents; yet this little voice piped up at all hours, early in the morning or late in the evening, "Mama? Mama? Go home tomorrow?" How puzzling! I had already learned that there were a few patients in the institution who were not of an advanced age—could it be that they took occasional children? (My thought must have been influenced by memory of the children's ward in Indian Hospital.) Finally I confided my puzzlement to Florence.

"That isn't a child," she said. "That's Annie. They say she has the mind of a four-year-old."

Gradually I learned more of Annie's story. She was an Indian woman from Winslow; therefore, I assume, an Apache. I never learned what her physical difficulty was, but heard she had been brought in in a very precarious condition. She sat all day in her wheelchair in the door of her room, except when she wheeled herself down to get a cigarette and afterwards to the TV Room. It seems strange that she was capable of this unsupervised activity, yet I met her once or twice in the corridor and saw her once sitting in the TV Room. She looked to be in her forties, probably her early forties. In repose, she had the saddest face that I have every seen, which occasionally broke into a really beautiful smile, marred only by terribly decayed teeth. Every passerby was addressed as "Mama." Sometimes a nurse would say, "Annie, are you going home tomorrow?" Then she would give that fantastically joyous smile and echo, "Winslow! Go home! Mama!"

The nurses and various other persons had given Annie a number of toys. When she sat in the doorway of her room, she usually held a battered teddy bear or a large doll in her arms. One day a passerby asked, "What's your baby's name?" With a look of inexpressible sadness and confusion, Annie responded, "I threw my baby away." This may have been literally true. Annie was said to have borne several children, whom her mother was raising. (It is not uncommon for Indian children to be raised by the grandmother, but this was surely an exceptionally tragic case.)

Annie had two distinct personalities. The hoarse, furious voice which cried after everyone who passed, "Go to hell! Son-a-bitch, go to hell!" took over on days when the sweet, childish treble was not heard. Several of the black aides would not go near her when this self was ascendant—or even when it wasn't, for their presence tended to call it forth. Annie spat at them and tore their uniforms, and they wanted no part of her; although a few claimed they knew how to handle her. It is a fact that racial bigotry is often rampant on Indian Reservations—and Annie was not inhibited in the expression of her feelings.

Florence had a daffodil-yellow dress which didn't entirely satisfy her. One day she said, "I believe I'll give this to Annie. The color will be becoming to her." No sooner said than done, and a few days later Annie wore it. But to our disappointment, the aide had put it on her backwards. Florence was one of the rare few who understood that even such a forlorn specimen of womanhood as Annie is entitled to beauty.

The woman whose ululations anticipated the dawn was one of Annie's roommates. The "girls" called her Emma, but certain of the nurses, with unwonted respect or affection, spoke of her as Mrs. Boucher. She was able, though unsighted, to propel her wheelchair up and down the corridor; and she must at least have been able to perceive light, for she frequently turned into open doors. When she came into our room, Lura addressed her with what sounded like a combination of fear and anger: "Scat! Shoo! Git out of here, you don't belong here!" If Mrs. Boucher was singing or making her inarticulate sounds (as she generally was), Lura said angrily, "Shut up! Stop that noise!" And when the intruder's wheelchair blocked her own exit, she became frantic. One of the "girls," in reply to my question, told me that when Emma moaned "Help me! Help me!" or made her plaintive, inarticulate noise she was suffering because her bowels were impacted; eventually someone would get around to giving her an enema.

The third occupant of that room was named Lillian. I first met her in the dining room. A handsome woman with a beautiful coiffure, she seemed at first sight one of the less handicapped; but when she spoke, a thin thread of saliva hung from her mouth. One Sunday when Lillian and I were seated at a table with the two black patients, I offended her by not finishing my portion of chicken. Lillian leaned over and appealed to the woman across from her, "Look at her! She's leaving all that good food! What's the matter with her?" The woman (I think she was the one called Mrs. Brown) at first ignored her, but when she persisted, drooling over her plate, she said shortly, "That's her business, not yours."

At that time Lillian's speech was coherent. She spoke an eastern-city dialect which sounded to me as if it might have originated in New Jersey. She was gregarious, always appeared at noonday dinner, and I think attended the Bingo games. One day, however, she began to tell everyone that her son was coming "next Tuesday" to take her back to Chicago. She said he had arranged to place her in a nursing home in the Chicago area (I believe she said the place was called Oak Park) where he could visit her daily. The story sounded so rational that she was generally believed by fellow patients and nurses' aides, although I suppose the nurses must have known better.

On Monday a number of persons told her good-bye. But Tuesday passed, and no son came to fetch her. There was no letter, telegram, or other communication. Lillian appeared no more in the dining room. Her voice was frequently heard calling, "Nurse! Nurse!"—as she pronounced it, it was almost "noice"— "I'll give you a dollar if you'll take me up the hill! Please! I'll give you five dollars!"

The occupants of the room directly across the hall from us were of an exceptionally high mental caliber. Nearest the door was Miss May Anderson. She had suffered a stroke two years before and had been a resident of Golden Mesa ever since. She, like Florence, was one of the fortunate ones whose relatives had not abandoned her. A devoted sister and brother-in-law came at least once a week. The sister always looked through her dresses (she had beautiful clothes) and took those which needed washing or altering. The brother-in-law brought little treats in the way of food—May detested the Nursing Home fare. If it had been possible for them to care for her, they would have gladly taken her home. May was confined to a wheelchair which held one leg extended, and one hand was helpless, or almost so. She was not responding to therapy.

It is possible that the Kramers had known Miss Anderson and her family before her hospitalization. Certainly they were now good friends, and there was much visiting back and forth.

The occupant of the middle bed was in her advanced eighties or early nineties, but she went everywhere unassisted, using her walker. Once when she came to our room, I said, "I wish I had the courage to go about as you do; but I'm afraid of falling." "I'm afraid too," she confided. "Every step I take, I'm afraid."

Nearest the window was a still older woman. May was impatient with her because she was deaf and very forgetful; but at that she exhibited a much slighter degree of senility than a large percentage of the patients.

Hilda, the woman who had threatened to make a disturbance in the beauty parlor, lived in a room a little farther out

towards the end of the East Wing. Hilda had been superinten-
dent of nurses in a large hospital. Now there was little left of
her former mental powers except the habit of domination.
Night and day she patrolled the corridor, attempting to assert
her nonexistent authority whenever she thought she saw an
opportunity. One evening I overhead her telling a new LVN,
"You may address me as Doctor." What did that reveal of
an unfulfilled ambition? Hilda bullied the girls as much as
they would allow, and not infrequently threatened physical
violence.

Once I asked a nurse, "Doesn't Hilda *ever* sleep?" "Oh,
yes," she replied. "She goes to sleep right after she has her
supper at five-thirty and sleeps soundly until eleven. Then she
gets up and walks."

Hilda had beautiful clothes, but as her mental faculties deteriorated she became averse to dressing properly. More and
more often she performed her phantom duties in her bath-
robe, although the nurses attempted to shame her into getting dressed. Once she appeared in the corridor in bra and
underpants. She resisted vigorously the attempt to hustle her
back to her room. "I intend to take a shower," she said with
dignity. Patients registered in advance to go on the various
outings which were occasionally offered. Once Hilda registered
for an excursion, but as the hour for departure approached,
she lay on her bed in her underwear. To all exhortations to
get dressed, she replied, "Later! Later!"

I never saw Hilda in the dining room. Perhaps it was beneath
her dignity to eat with the other patients. But there was another, very undignified side to her nature. She was a klepto-
maniac. I was warned to watch my belongings; and periodically a nurse went through her things and returned trinkets to
their owners. Once I was shown a salvaged teddy bear—Annie's
perhaps, but more likely belonging to some elderly lady who
liked to dress her bed in schoolgirl fashion with dolls and
stuffed animals.

When I protested that I had nothing anyone would want,
I was told, "You'd be surprised at what they'll take." The in-
definite, impersonal "they" included all the light-fingered

and potentially light-fingered elderly—a category from which I felt myself not excluded in the nurses' eyes. Generalities were the rule. When I mentioned having written two books, nurses and aides instinctively classified me as an old woman who thought she had written two books—not very different from poor Lillian, who had deluded herself into believing that her son was coming for her Tuesday; or for that matter, from Hilda, who much of the time believed that she was still in an executive position.

Who were Hilda's roommates? I never sorted them out, but I'm quite sure she could not have shared a room with another dominant personality. I shudder to think what would have happened if she and Lura had been together.

Mr. Naha also was located up in that part of the East Wing. I saw him at mealtimes and cigarette times patiently and literally inching his way along towards the dining room or the nurses' station. He never mastered the navigation of a wheel-chair. Perhaps his fingers were unable to grasp the steel rims which enable the sitter to propel himself forward. Nor was he able to walk himself along, as a number of the old men did. His fingers closed around the tire and imparted little or no forward motion. He pulled himself along by the waist-high railing when it was available, but in passing open doors or other spaces where there was no railing he proceeded by painful forward jerks of his body, not speaking, not asking for help, his deeply lined Indian face expressing patience and indestructible dignity. Lura was deeply contemptuous of anyone who could not zip about in a wheelchair as easily as she could. Once, with a mixture of pity and exasperation, she attempted briefly to instruct Mr. Naha. "Here! Don't put your hands that way! Grab hold of it here! It's easy!" she shouted at him, as people are apt to do in trying to communicate with those who may not understand English. Mr. Naha, bewildered no doubt by what must have seemed an unprovoked attack, looked at her in uncomprehending silence; and Lura took herself off, muttering angrily.

The "girls" addressed Mr. Naha disrespectfully as Charlie,

but the nurses for the most part called him Mr. Naha. One of them told me he was a "chief" in one of the pueblos. Certainly he was not abandoned. Infrequently an impressive-looking man, holding a wide-brimmed Stetson hat, stood beside him and conversed. He spoke and Mr. Naha answered. I could not hear their words, and have no idea if Mr. Naha spoke English or Spanish in addition to his native tongue, whatever that may have been. Once, passing him in the corridor, I tried him out with, *"Buenas tardes, señor."* He did not return the salutation. I did have the impression that the young women, probably granddaughters or nieces, who came to visit him spoke Spanish. They came in a group of three or four, handsome women with loose black hair, one of them carrying an infant; and they never failed to wheel him up and down the corridor. I think he enjoyed these rides, which were in such contrast to his usual painful progress. It must have been these contacts with his own people which prevented Mr. Naha from choosing Willie Mike's way of escape.

Once Mr. Naha was seated at the same table with me in the dining room. I did not care for my dessert—I think it was a piece of cake—but I noted the relish with which Mr. Naha ate his and the sudden gleam in his eye as he glanced at my untouched portion. Timorously, I offered it to him. His face lit up, and he nodded his thanks. After that, if he sat at the same table, or at an adjoining one where I could tap him on the shoulder to attract his attention, I always gave him my dessert, whether or not I could have eaten it myself. This was the least I could do for a fellow sufferer towards whom my heart yearned.

The most deliberately callous act I witnessed in Golden Mesa had Mr. Naha as its victim. I was progressing painfully in my wheelchair towards the little ramp by the nurses' station; Mr. Naha sat hopelessly at its foot. His mode of locomotion was difficult enough on the level; he simply could not manage the slighest ascent. Two nurses' aides came swinging blithely along, deep in conversation. One was a stranger to me, the other was named Lois, a slender girl with straight blonde hair and a quantity of blue eyeshadow. (The black aide who worked mostly in The Ward and adjoining rooms was called Big Lois to distinguish her from this other Lois.) I heard the "girls" say, "Charlie," not in salutation but with amusement. As they swept past, Lois turned and took hold of the handles of Mr. Naha's wheelchair. Feeling the incipient motion, his face lit up with incredulous gratitude. He really thought that he was about to be pushed up the ramp. Instead, Lois swung his chair askew in the corridor and went on, laughing. Before, I had been inclined to like Lois; now I felt that if she should be assigned to our room I would be ill with disgust.

I don't know who Mr. Naha's roommates were. One might have been a man called Bill, a longtime resident of Phoenix, whom Mike and Florence knew very well. Bill appeared to be a very normal man from the waist up, but I was told that his legs, covered by a blanket, were horribly deformed by some bone disease. During my stay I noticed that he became markedly less social. Florence said that after his wife died, he had "just given up."

The only other resident of that area who stands out is Mrs. Forrest. She was supplementing her major income by selling Avon products. To have an Avon lady calling gave a nice touch of commonplace, suburban reality, and it was pleasant to buy a lipstick or a small jar of cream sachet. The only drawback was that Mrs. Forrest was deaf as a post. She wore a hearing aid, but apparently her hearing had gone beyond the point where it could be aided. This made business transactions difficult almost to the point of impossibility. I classified her with the mentally undeteriorated, until one day when some artificial roses were stolen from her room. She went into a typically senile tantrum, and harped on the matter loudly at dinner time for days. I thought, How long before I go that way?

When I walked up the corridor with Dorothy, I looked into two or three rooms where the shades were perpetually drawn and old women lay in their beds in the fetal position. This too filled me with foreboding. Was I even now beginning

to slip downhill? I had to admit to myself that I was now resigned to using the bedpan at night—it even seemed pleasanter
and certainly much easier to have a bedpan slipped under me
than to struggle up onto a commode as I had so gladly done
in Lake Havasu Community Hospital. . . .

Down the corridor in the other direction, there were a few
rooms between Room 36 and the nurses' station. In one of
these, the nearest, I think, lived two very deaf ladies who had
a television set and kept it on full blast. Sometime after I was
settled in, on an evening when the noise level in the corridor
happened to drop somewhat, I heard a voice of a newscaster re-
ferring to Mrs. Betty Ford's mastectomy, and going on to mention President Ford. This was how I learned that Richard Nixon
had been in some manner deposed from his Imperial Presi-
dency. Time was still to elapse before I would know how this
had come about. Later, wheeling myself past the room with
the perpetual broadcast, I saw that the occupants had a very
small color TV set, possibly a Sony. Immediately some treach-
erous portion of my mind began to wonder if I could not af-
ford to buy myself such a set and to plan how it could be
placed in the room so that I would have sole control over it.
It would be more practical to have a very small TV set than to
try to secure the transportation of the larger table model I already owned. These thoughts and plans were part of an insid-
ious acceptance of the possibility of permanent residence in
Golden Mesa. Gratefully permitting myself to be settled for
the night, I sometimes wondered if, along with my conscious
determination to resist, to retain at all costs my position in the
land of the living, there was not beginning to run a subcon-
scious acceptance of this Limbo-like existence. Vi had said that
I might stay "for the rest of my life", and when Lura made
her confused statements about staying overnight because it
was "too late to go home" an aide always responded, "This is
your home." Remembering these things, I would feel a chill
of horror, I would rouse myself from the dream of "staying"
as vigorously as I roused my mind from the not infrequent
temptation to drift into pleasantly incoherent dreams.

It really wouldn't have been so bad to contemplate permanent residence if I had had the money to live in the style of the woman just beyond the room with the color TV set. She had the whole room to herself and had furnished it with furniture brought from her home—from the hallway I saw a comfortable green velour sofa and matching armchair. Rumor had it that she had around-the-clock special nurses in attendance. And I am sure *her* doctor was not invisible.

Below the ramp, on the opposite side of the corridor, a man lived whom I feared a great deal more than I feared Hilda. Actually, Hilda inspired me with a sort of mild uneasiness which might have become fear if she had noticed me, which she never did. Not so with Hank. He would zoom up to me in his wheelchair, insist upon shaking hands, leer at me, tilt his hand up to his mouth in a convivial gesture, perhaps pat me on the knee; then zoom off again to my very great relief. Hank was, I believe, at least potentially ambulatory. He was fastened into his chair, perhaps to protect him from the possibility of falling, perhaps merely to make him more manageable. This part of his confinement he did not seem to mind. He sent the chair flying along at a great speed with thrusts of his powerful arms, and like Lura, would brook no obstacle. A slow-moving wheelchair which happened to get in his way would be swiftly shoved off to one direction or another. Hank was not an aged man. His mind had given way under some experience or combination of experiences undergone in World War II. I have no idea why he wasn't in a Veterans Hospital. He was said to have a wife and children. The wife (so I heard) came to see him occasionally, or at any rate came to collect his clothes for washing; the children (now long out on their own, assuming they had been born before the war) never came. Hank never ate from food presented to him on a tray, but snatched bits of food from other people's trays or from trays on the rack awaiting distribution. He was unbelievably quick, and went about with a wild, puckish grin on his face. Also he had an outrageous sense of humor and played practical jokes. Once passing a stack of diapers fresh from the laundry, he snatched one from the top, urinated on it, and thrust it back into the pile.

Hank never spoke except when an attempt was made to touch him physically. It took two aides to shave him, and the insertion of a suppository was a horrendous experience. At such times he became highly vocal, yelling curses and protests. "God damn you! Keep your hands offa me! Jesus Christ! What kind of a hospital *is* this? It's a Goddamn prison!" Once when taking Hank from his room to a shower stall, Callie left him sitting in a bath chair in the corridor just outside the TV Room. (Callie seems to have had a penchant for leaving her charges at critical times—perhaps that was part of the work-ing-two-jobs-at-once syndrome.) Hank, of course, was wearing only a sheet with his bare bottom hanging out of the hole in the chair. I was parked in my wheelchair by the nurses' sta-tion, waiting, futilely as usual, to attempt a long-distance call. Whether in resentment of the coming ordeal or from sheer deviltry, Hank defecated. It must have required considerable effort, for he produced a very small turd for so large a man. Callie came back and took him away, and wheelchair traffic began to cross and recross the small brown mound. *No one noticed.* Finally I attracted the attention of a passing nurse, and she notified housekeeping.

I mulled over Hank and his condition until my imagination had constructed an explanation, satisfactory to me though perhaps far from the truth. I imagined that Hank had been wounded and hospitalized in one of those dreadful places that specialized in human experimentation. This seemed to me a way of accounting for his reluctance to eat the food served him, his efforts at camaraderie with fellow "inmates," and his refusal to speak except in screaming terror when an attempt was made to lay hands on him.

Larry was a double amputee. I think he may have been one of Hank's roommates. I first noticed him in the dining room, collecting slices of uneaten bread, opening the outside doors and tossing the crumbled bits to birds in the parking lot. This seemed to me a harmless pursuit, although at intervals a nurse would make vigorous attempts to put a stop to it. She never succeeded. When Larry's bread was taken away from him, he patiently collected more and continued to feed the small twittering birds hopping about the parking lot and patio. He was no more than middle-aged, and I think in full possession of his faculties. There can't be much wrong with the mind of a person who likes to feed birds. I would have liked to have talked with Larry, but he ignored me. He was not gregarious.

Another man in the room with Hank was bedridden. I never saw him, but sometimes in the morning he made ululating plaints similar to Mrs. Boucher's. The "girls" said he was worse to take care of than Hank, because he spat at them, and he could spit a long way. And on the other side of the corridor I once saw an old man lying virtually naked (his hospital gown was up around his neck), screaming, "Nurse! Nurse! Somebody please help me!" Such pleas were routinely ignored. If you were in trouble, you pressed your call button and a light came on over the door, which might or might not bring assistance. If you couldn't reach the button or didn't have the mental ability to use it, you were out of luck. When I asked one of the "girls" about the man who seemed to be suffering so severely, she answered matter-of-factly, "Yes, his catheter needed fixing."

Mrs. Delacourt lived in the older part of the East Wing where the rooms were smaller, containing only two beds. She was a person with a son and daughter-in-law who came to see her at rather frequent intervals (at least the daughter-in-law did; the son was a preacher, busy with church duties). Mrs. Delacourt had her own wheelchair, with her name stencilled across the back. She was a sprightly, friendly creature, with a pronounced dowager's hump, which probably interfered with her balance. But she could walk with one four-pronged cane if Dorothy held her other arm, and she was capable of getting herself in and out of the wheelchair. After the noonday meal she wheeled herself out in a great hurry, went to her room and used the bathroom, and was on the way back to the Music Room across from the dining room to socialize with her friends before I had propelled myself halfway back to Room 36. That meant that she passed me twice and always exchanged a cheerful greeting.

At dinner Mrs. Delacourt, her roommate (a large and positive-looking woman), Mrs. Forrest, and a woman known to me only as Ellen always endeavored to share a table. Ellen was a handsome woman with close-cropped, well-groomed hair, very intelligent, not deaf, but not interested in making new acquaintances. She merely stared in silence on the one or two occasions when I tried to address her. In spite of having one leg extended straight out, she maneuvered herself well. Twice room was made at their table for a guest and a tray brought for Mrs. Delacourt's roommate's daughter. This very pregnant young woman had a four-year-old daughter, whose presence delighted many of the diners. Many of us were starved for contact with youth, and we heartily envied the grandmother. The child's mother brought a honeydew melon for the grandmother, and I eyed from afar the mouth-watering slice.

A few nights after this happy visit there was a good bit of noise and confusion in the corridor, and a shortage of "girls" to answer call lights. In the morning we learned that Mrs. Delacourt's roommate had died in the night. Evidently, there had not been time to take her to a hospital. She had gone through her death agony just a few feet from Mrs. Delacourt, who had been her roommate for a long time and loved her dearly. Next day Mrs. Delacourt's eyes were streaming. "I cried all night," she said, "and now I can't seem to stop crying."

Not long after she suffered another severe blow. It came following a few hours of great elation. One day she went about confiding to everyone in the dining room and corridor, "I saw my doctor, and he says there isn't a thing wrong with me. He says I'm really in remarkably good condition. He says there isn't any physical reason why I can't *go home*. I'm going to phone my son. I'm going to have him come and get me *right away*."

The phone call was a local one and eventually she got to make it. Next day she reported, somewhat crestfallen but still full of hope, "I couldn't get hold of my son. I finally talked to Catherine—that's my daughter-in-law. I'm sure she'll come and get me right away."

Catherine came and visited with Mrs. Delacourt in the dining room—the son, damn him, quite evidently lacked even a pinch of moral courage. Catherine was a typical drab, harassed fundamentalist preacher's wife, walking heavily and carrying a large string bag, full of God knows what. She explained reasonably to her mother-in-law that both she and James (or whatever his name was) were far too busy to take proper care of her. She was much better off right here in Golden Mesa, where she could have every attention. But she promised, indeed they both promised faithfully, that they would come and get her Christmas Day and she could *spend all day* with the family. After all, she said brightly, it was only a little more than two months till Christmas.

This time Mrs. Delacourt's eyes streamed for days on end. But she was a proud woman. She said she must have gotten some sort of eye infection.

Mrs. Delacourt's spirit was wounded but she did not break as Lillian had. After all, there were those much worse off than either she or I. When I walked with Dorothy Williams to the east end of the corridor, passing those perpetually darkened rooms, I sometimes caught the unmistakable sickening odor of cancer; and once, passing Annie in the hall, I imagined a whiff of that same odor.

5

The first arranged outing that I knew anything about was a proposed trip to the Zoo, courtesy of the young people of The Church of Jesus Christ of Latter Day Saints. These kindly Mormon youths had vans that would transport wheelchair patients and strong young arms to help with the lifting. Crystal and Ann Keim both urged me to register for the tour, but I refused. I felt too much like a caged animal myself to enjoy looking at other caged animals.

Besides at that time I did not feel it would be possible to make a single effort beyond the response required by daily and inescapable routines. I did not feel up to being lifted and hauled about. It would be a year and a half after I left Golden Mesa before I understood the reason for that inertia, that dreadful and (at the time) inexplicable malaise. I had no idea that I was seriously ill, suffering not only from a completely deteriorated hip but from two large hiatal hernias, digestive organs displaced into the chest cavity, and pressure on one lung. I shouldn't, according to all reason, have been alive, and I was actually staying alive by a combination of ignorance, faith, and will—and just possibly by the mystic power of an as yet unfulfilled destiny. As it was, I put my continuing nausea down to the aftereffects of the gallbladder operation, and castigated myself for lack of energy and ambition.

When the excursionists came back they reported a marvelous time, including free soft drinks and sandwiches; but I felt no regrets about remaining in my room.

The next diversion was to be a "Watermelon Bust" in the patio. I didn't think I wanted to go to that either, mainly because the patio was even farther away than the dining room, and the exertion of wheeling myself loomed as an insurmountable ordeal. But Crystal promised to take me and to see that I was safely returned to my room by the time the evening "girls" arrived.

The patio proved to be a place of sheer delight. There was a covered asphalt area with tables, and there were trees shading an unkempt lawn that in its very roughness gave an intimation of freedom. The melons were luscious, ripe to the point of perfection, and ice cold. (Because of showery weather, it had been necessary to postpone the feast for a week, but the fruit had not deteriorated.) The region around Phoenix is preeminently fine melon-growing country—I had not tasted such melons since my Texas childhood.

Florence was there, and her husband with her. And Annie was there, very quiet and well-behaved. Looking at her, I thought of the phrase from Psalms, "I have quieted myself like a weaned child." (Later, at the September birthday party, she drank her punch and ate her cake with perfect decorum.) Lura, inexplicably, refused vehemently to go. I couldn't understand this, for she loved to eat and enjoyed going about in her wheelchair.

I sat at a table with Señora Moreno. Her face was beautifully chiseled, aristocratic; and she had the most erect carriage of any patient in the Nursing Home. She wore modest gold hoops in her pierced ears and a large gold wedding band. Her demeanor was reserved though her face brightened when I spoke to her in Spanish, and she made a courteous rejoinder. She might have been a highborn Mexican lady. It was later, in the dining room, that she told me of her life of constant toil as a miner's wife and widow. There is an innate aristocracy that is not dependent upon worldy fortunes. I will not say it has no basis in birth. The Indian and Spanish strains which mingled in her heritage may have been equally distinguished.

From that time on I could not get enough of the patio. Sometimes Mike took Florence and then came back for me. After I became acquainted with Elaine Haase and her mother, Elaine frequently came for me—in the goodness of her heart, she made herself responsible for the transportation of several persons who found it difficult to wheel themselves so far.

Marie Haase was in Golden Mesa solely for the purpose of recuperating from a broken hip. She was a transient, and knew she was a transient, and her daughter came to see her almost daily. Therefore she was not unduly depressed by her surroundings. For her, the dreadful void that I could not bear to contemplate did not exist. She was a little deaf, and conversation did not always flow smoothly. But when I found that she had recently returned from Europe and could talk intelligently about her trip, I made every effort to make myself understood. Then I met Elaine, an alert, no-nonsense person, and a devoted daughter in her brisk, unsentimental way. Elaine and her mother were active in Eastern Star. Elaine occupied her hands, while she sat in the patio with me, making stick horses for a charity sale or bazaar. My daughter Georgia was also a Past Matron, though no longer active since tribal affairs had come to absorb all her energies. This gave me, if not even a tenuous connection, at least a sympathetic understanding of the Masonic Lodge and its allied institutions. Elaine was employed in the financial department of the Maricopa County Hospital. It was from her that I first learned of the law by which Arizona could take *all* an indigent patient's Social Security check.

The Haases had a friend called Lucy in the Medicare Section. She suffered terribly from arthritis. Pain kept her awake day and night, except when she could sit in the warmth of the sun. Every day she dozed in her chair until we had all left. I understand that an aide always came to take her back to her room before nightfall. I hope this was true. Other patients of varying mental capacity came and went in the patio. I vaguely remember a woman who usually had her finger marking her place in a book, and who conversed intelligently but—perhaps for that reason—established no intimacy with the rest of us. And I recall another woman (or was it the same one?) who spoke of hunting trips she and her husband had taken by plane to Mexico and of the vast numbers of quail they had shot—at which I always flinched inwardly.

But it was not the people who frequented the patio that constituted its attraction for me. With the exception of a very few, I would have preferred their absence. It was the area outside the asphalted space that enthralled me. Trees (nameless to me, with dark or olive green leaves) grew randomly on the sparse scraggly patch of grass, hardly tended enough to be called a lawn. Small brown birds hopped and twittered in the grass, or suddenly in small groups flew up and perched in the trees. (On some afternoons Larry cleverly got himself through the heavy doors at the end of the corridor and tossed his crumbs to these little birds—whereupon they all flew down and vied with each other noisily for a few moments. Then, without exchanging a word with anyone, he went back quickly indoors.) On the low adobe wall which partially closed off this refuge, tiny brown lizards (I believe Elaine called them chameleons) sunned themselves in absolute immobility or darted about with a swiftness the eye could scarcely follow. And overhead, of course, arched that high, indescribably blue desert sky, always seemingly undimmed by Phoenix smog.

I think I have always loved beauty suggested to the imagination almost as well as beauty seen. When my parents and I returned from our first trip to Mexico (Old Mexico, we always called it), the September after I had turned fourteen, I remember walking with a feeling of strangeness and emptiness in the dusty backyard where I had played for most of my childhood. Then I saw a bright red leaf (I didn't know at the time that the color was due to disease) on a stunted peach tree, and suddenly it was as if I had looked on beauty's face. In Mexico I had seen my first real mountains, and had been appropriately awed and enthralled, but always with a certain reservation—as if somewhere there must be higher mountains, grander vistas, views more inspiring, speaking more directly to the soul. Now I realized, and tried silently and vainly to put into words, that the mountains I had strained towards were mountains dreamed or imagined, scenes that never were and never could be of this world. In somewhat similar fashion, the patio of Golden Mesa solaced me, not by what it really was, but by suggesting the vast deserts, the indescribably lush oases, the exotic fauna which a mere human might never know because these imaginings existed only in the transcendent universe of the dreamer and the seer.

When Rosita, the soft-voiced, pretty Apache girl who was the social worker employed by the Bureau of Indian Affairs to visit Indians living in rest homes in that area, came to me in Room 36, glanced doubtfully at the Kramers and Lura, and asked if there was some place we could talk privately, I at once suggested the patio. She wheeled me there, and chose, with proper deference to my desires, a table remote from other persons taking the air. I liked, even loved, Rosita at first sight, but I also knew intuitively that she had been sent less to check on my welfare than to secure my Social Security check for officialdom. Circuitously she broached the subject. With great firmness I stated that I had never signed any paper except one that made my medical records available, and that I had been assured both by the head doctor and the Bureau of Indian Affairs social worker at Indian Hospital in Parker that my stay in Golden Mesa would be absolutely without expense to myself. Rosita, with relief, turned to more congenial matters. Mr. Naha, she said, con-

sidered me "a very nice lady." It warmed my heart to know
that his reserve was due to shyness, not latent enmity. After
this, when we met in the corridor, I smiled at him and saluted
him warmly in Spanish or English, whichever came to mind
(I never learned if he understood either language). He never
answered in words. His face, engraved by centuries of dignity
and self-control, never actually broke into a smile. But nonetheless there was an inward glow, a moment of psychic com-
munion which I think cheered us both.

Later Rosita brought me an application for Supplemental
Social Security Income, already made out, which she said Mr.
King wanted me to sign. Again I said that I had already sent
in such an application while I resided in Poway and it would
only confuse the issue to mail in a second one. Again with
relief Rosita accepted dismissal of the subject. We went out
onto the patio for a long and pleasant visit. I admired her
beautiful silver and turquoise jewelry, and she told me a little
about her background and then launched into a description of
the Apache Sunrise Dance, the beautiful and lavish rite of passage which marked a young girl's entrance into womanhood.

When a girl was about thirteen, Rosita said, the parents, if
they were able to bear the expense, gave this dance in her
honor. It lasted for four nights. There were lavish presents for
everyone, and the girl herself danced all night every night,
and everyone honored her.

By now I perceived a definite attack on my Social Security
income. I spoke cautiously about it to someone, I believe it
was Ann Keim, and she replied with equal caution that she
thought the rules were a little different for nursing homes
than they were for Indian hospitals. Sometime previous to
this my mind had cleared sufficiently to enable me to deal intelligently with the small bundle of correspondence which
Mary Mitchell had brought to me in Parker. A letter which
I had thrust aside as something official and quite beyond my
comprehension proved to be a check for seventy-three dollars,
reimbursing me for a percentage of the price of prescription

drugs I had bought in Los Angeles and Poway. The check was already two months old and I felt that I should cash it immediately. But although I had a few checks left in my checkbook, I had no more deposit slips. I could clearly visualize the little red cardboard box containing checks and deposit slips imprinted with my name lying safely in the top drawer of my desk in Chemehuevi Valley. They might as well have been on the mountains of the moon. I wrote to the bank in Needles, explaining my temporary location and asking that additional deposit slips be sent directly to me. No reply. (The slips were sent promptly—to our post office box at Havasu Lake! Eventually they were forwarded or brought to me.) I talked my dilemma over with Ann Keim and decided to sign the check and deposit the cash in the office of Golden Mesa, where I already had some twenty or thirty dollars. We agreed the money would be safe there. No doubt it was—but I never saw any of it.

I was getting uneasy about the financial situation. I had the feeling that if I fended off his gentle deputy's approach for one more month, the redoubtable Mr. King would appear in person, and that would be the last I would see of my Social Security checks.

One afternoon when I went to the patio I found the patients who were already there, including Florence, in a state of excitement over an incident which everyone described, with a not unpleasurable thrill, as dreadful. As nearly as I could gather, a newcomer to Golden Mesa had leaned so far forward in his wheelchair, struggling against his restraints, that someone, a kindhearted visitor or ambulatory patient, had feared he would fall on his face and had attempted to help him right himself. Whereupon the newcomer, with superhuman strength, had picked up a large container filled with sand (for the dousing of cigarette butts) and hurled it at the would-be good samaritan, who fortunately had been able to dodge. The offender had now been removed, but the animated buzz of conversation continued through a good part of the afternoon.

I asked what the man looked like, and was informed that his appearance was terrible.

A day or so later I met a man whom I had not seen before being pushed along in a wheelchair. His hair stood up every which way and his wide open blue eyes stared wildly. I never saw him again. In this instance, discretion must have prevailed over cupidity, with the result that this particular madman had been removed to a more secure environment. (All things considered, I must say in fairness to Golden Mesa that the mad people it housed, even poor Hank, were not truly dangerous; Hilda was potentially threatening, but Annie did not have the strength really to hurt anyone—except possibly a black aide who ventured too close when the violent side of her personality was dominant.)

During my afternoons in the patio, I saw, although I did not actually become acquainted with, a frail, stoop-shouldered elderly woman who was indefatigable in her helpfulness. She spent much time wheeling patients who could not easily propel themselves. I think it was Elaine Haase who told me that this woman's husband was a patient, confined to his bed and hopelessly ill. She came everyday to do what she could for him and to keep him company; and when he fell asleep or needed to be quiet, she devoted herself to other patients.

Counterbalancing the greed and hyprocisy of management— advertising great solicitude for the aged while skimping unmercifully on such essentials as food and the quality of help; the callousness and incompetence of some of the underpaid assistants; and the despairing self-centeredness of many patients—were other less conspicuous human qualities: helpfulness exhibited by those themselves in need of help; touches of humanity displayed by hurried and overworked aides; and small courtesies shown by sufferers whose sufferings could not extinguish gentleness, unquenchable and universal love, and solicitude.

Elaine Haase did not confine her care to her own mother. Several of us came to depend upon her to wheel us to and

from the patio. Also she could be imposed upon to do errands
outside the confines of the Nursing Home. Towards the end
of my stay she even made a long-distance call for me.

There were two routes to the patio. One was by the way of
the large nurses' station where cigarettes were distributed,
turning left where the corridors forked instead of right to the
dining room, and following along another corridor to a pair
of heavy doors—at least they looked heavy and forbidding to
me. The other way led more directly out into the fresh air.
One could open the outside door in the TV (or smoking)
Room, pass directly out onto a cement walk, and turn right
towards the patio. Once when I saw the prison pallor of Lura's
face through a blue haze of smoke, I could not resist asking
her one more time to come out into the sunlight. Elaine added
her urgings to mine. Lura declined with an emphasis that
seemed more like fear than rage. "No! No! Git that door shut!"
Remembering her professed penchant for fresh air, this
seemed to me very curious. I recalled one night when the noise
in the corridor had been considerably worse than usual. One
of the Chicano aides, a woman named Juanita, older than
most of the "girls" and very kind and courteous, came in to
give me the bedpan and asked if I wouldn't like the door
closed for awhile. I said "by all means." No sooner was it
done, than the ever-wakeful Lura proclaimed that we were all
going to smother to death. With my usual foolish and futile
attempt to reason with her, I responded that the air came
through the air-conditioning vents, and that the air in the corridor was probably staler than that in our room. Not so, Lura
averred; that doorway was our only source of oxygen. I myself tend to have what is currently described as "a thing"
about closed doors. I don't as a rule like them. But at the moment (the time was about 3:00 a.m.) a little less noise and
glare seemed desirable. I ignored Lura, which is what I should
have done from the start, and kept quiet, hoping she would
soon forget about the door and go back to her usual monologue. There was nothing she could do about it, I thought,

since either through ignorance or stubborness she never pressed her call button. To my amazement she suddenly reversed her position in bed and draped herself over the foot of the bed like an aged monkey hanging by its tail. Defying gravity, she extended her body horizontally until she succeeded in grasping the doorknob and flinging the door open. Then, muttering in satisfaction, she once again sat upright and went into a long monologue concerning "some people's" aversion to fresh air.

I mentioned this episode to Elaine. "She doesn't even want this door closed for a second—why won't she ever go out into the patio?"

"Don't you know?" Elaine replied. "She's afraid of getting lost."

Recalling Lura's waking nightmare about piloting her wheelchair through the streets of downtown Phoenix, I had to agree, at least partially. "But sometimes she talks about going home," I protested, remembering her not infrequent threat: "I'll have my sister come get me in the morning."

"They all say that," Elaine replied calmly.

Florence had assured me that Lura really did have a sister and a niece. Once they had come to see her with reasonable regularity, and Lura had been much better mentally. She had done very nice crocheting and had been less subject to delusion. Now, though she had no realization of the elapsed time since she had last seen her relatives, their continued absence accelerated the separation from reality. A nurse who had not been employed in Golden Mesa for a year came back to visit and said, "Lura, I need some more crocheted edging for pillow cases. You do such nice work—can you make me some?" And Lura had responded uncertainly, "Maybe so. I guess so, if you got me a real simple pattern."

Still there was her routine statement, made almost every evening, "I was going to go home. But it's so late and I'm tired. I guess I'll stay here all night." To which an aide invariably replied soothingly, "This *is* your home." (God in heaven! How long before someone would say that to me? And would

I come to accept it as true? In a certain sense it was as true for me even now as it was for Lura; because I could see no feasible way for me to live anywhere else.)

Happily, Lura's sister did come to see her eventually. They went to the dining room together and a tray was brought for the sister. And after that Lura seemed a little less determined to confine herself to Room 36, the adjacent corridor, and the TV Room. She went as far as the dining room on her own initiative, but never, never out into the patio. Walls which once might have seemed restrictive of freedom now gave her her only security.

6

The Music Room, across the corridor from the dining room, had large picture windows looking out onto what must have been the main parking lot. (Perhaps it was this proximity to the outside world which deterred Lura from coming here.) Seated in this room, one could observe the occasional arrival of ambulances and watch nurses and nurses' aides scurrying back and forth to their cars. We also saw visitors come and go, including those anxious-faced middle-aged persons who were inspecting Golden Mesa for the purpose of locating a suitable place for the parent or grandparent who had just become too much for them to continue to cope with at home.

Visitors came directly from the parking lot into the smallish, pleasant lobby which adjoined the Music Room. Everything about the lobby was calculated to give an agreeable first impression. There were comfortable seats and always a large bouquet of flowers, usually plastic, like the indestructible, synthetically cheery little bouquets that decked every table in the dining room, but sometimes actually fresh. (I always suspected the latter of arriving via the graveside of a deceased patient.)

It was in the lobby that I visited with my Indian friends the Antones when they drove from Chemehuevi Valley to Phoenix to consult a doctor in the large Phoenix Indian Hos-

pital about a persistent rash on Angie's foot which had evidently proven too much for the diagnostic facilities at Parker.
They knew of my whereabouts from Georgia and kindly
looked in on me before driving home. Several nurses passed
through and saw us together. They had also seen Georgia when
she came to see me soon after my arrival, making a journey
which had proven entirely too arduous and painful to be repeated. Now these nurses made a point of telling me that it
was "so nice" my daughter could visit me again. Apparently
to the untrained Caucasian eye all Indians, like all Orientals,
look alike.

The anxious seekers who came to Golden Mesa were duly
reassured by the charming entry way. Husband and wife might
murmur to one another, "You see, dear, it isn't in the least
like those dreadful places we read about." "No, indeed, everything looks very homelike." Then the Grasshopper Lady in
person would give them a tour of the institution, pointing out
desirable features: the bright rooms, the well-made beds with
their attractive colored spreads, the cheerful dining room
which was also a social hall, and the various recreational facilities. Along with the tour-guide patter came the hypnotically
repeated assurance, "I'm sure he (or she, or they) will adjust
nicely and be very happy here." Eventually the relatives would
be convinced, heave sighs of relief, or helplessness; stifle the
last qualms of conscience, or make a bad and uneasy bargain
with it; and go into the office to complete the financial arrangements.

Returning to the Music Room, I should explain that it de-
rived its name from the presence of a battered, out-of-tune
upright piano. Occasionally one of the deafer "inmates" would
bang out something upon this instrument with all the force
her feeble arms could muster, holding down the "loud pedal"
(as my peers and I called it seventy years ago) while arthritic
fingers struck any number of wrong notes. As a rule the piano
was silent except when expounders of religious doctrine or
groups of entertainers visited us. Patients congregated in this
room merely to enjoy each other's company. Perhaps "enjoy"

is too strong a word. What brought them together was, more likely, merely that herding impulse which, according to anthropologist Colin Turnbull, prompts even the antisocial Ik to sit in proximity to one another at certain times. The harmony of these Music Room gatherings was frequently marred by competition for wheelchair space facing the windows.

Here we were entertained when visitors from other rest homes or nursing facilities came to show off their talents. There was a performance by a "kitchen band." One of the visitors played the piano while the others earnestly rubbed on washboards or banged pans or did whatever they were supposed to do on various utensils more or less in unison. The ladies were not spectacularly costumed, although I believe they wore housedresses; but the men sported the kind of straw hats affected by small-town dudes circa 1910, and a few were in shirt-sleeves with suspenders. One gentleman (perhaps he was the conductor) had on a pink striped shirt with elastic garters on his sleeves.

The "kitchen band" was sufficiently distressing, but even more ghastly were the hula dancers. Mercifully, the ancient skinny (or flabby) bodies were not nude under their grass skirts and artificial leis. All wore some sort of tights and sweat shirts. Their energetic leader had on what must have been a bright red leotard, although it closely resembled a suit of old-fashioned long red-flannel underwear—which I'm sure would have been much too hot. This lady was teacher of the group and inspirer of the whole project. She had recently returned from a trip to The Islands, and obviously was residing in a rest home more because she found it convenient than from necessity. She earnestly assured us that, with a little effort, we all could attain the degree of grace and agility exhibited by her and her pupils. (I would have been satisfied to have been able to walk across the room without a walker.)

These various performances were staged to inspire us, to shake us out of our respective sloughs of discouragement. In reality they had the opposite effect. After the exhibition of hula dancing, I asked a fellow sufferer, "Did you enjoy it?"

"I might have," she replied, "if they'd been young like they're supposed to be. I don't like to see old people make fools of themselves."

It was almost as though there was a conspiracy to banish thoughts and memories of youth and springtime. Just as all the pictures were autumnal, the persons who came to entertain us were virtually all aged. The one exception was a group of Lutheran young people, ranging in age from ten to eighteen, who came to sing and read from the Scriptures. They went from room to room like troubadours one evening after we had been bedded down for the night. The fresh young faces and fresh young voices were delightful; but the reading was from a modern version of the Bible, which for some reason always sets my teeth on edge. I asked the eighteen-year-old reader, after I had thanked him properly, why he preferred a modern translation; and he responded earnestly that it was much easier to understand. (I know little about Lutheran doctrine and nothing about Lutheran services; when I come to think of it, I don't know if they have ever used the King James Version, whose lyric thunder I have loved from infancy. I now resolved that if ever again I got my hands on such a Bible, I would memorize pages of Psalms.)

The last time I visited the Music Room was to view an exhibit of "old-time" cars. This actually took place in the parking lot, but those of us who were confined to wheelchairs and therefore exempt from being dragged out, more or less willingly, to ride in one of the motley collection of vehicles assembled for the occasion were allowed to watch from indoors. This was supposedly a costume party. Such parties were dear to the hearts of the powers who governed Golden Mesa—I presume they made good advertising copy. A number of the bewildered old people in wheelchairs were decked out in odds and ends of ancient finery, and some of the chairs had bright colored balloons tied to them. Some of the staff also were in costume, including, on this occasion, the Grasshopper Lady. I looked up to see a tall figure (she always looked tall to me from my wheelchair, but I don't know if she actually was) wearing a long, high-waisted white gown with long, full sleeves.

Her face, peering out from inside a very fancy white bonnet tied under the chin with wide white streamers, looked less predatory, softer, more feminine; and her figure, with knobby arms and legs well hidden, was quite unrecognizable. In short, she presented a very attractive appearance—a woman born out of her time, at least as regards becoming adornment! The costume was something of an anachronism; as nearly as I could judge it looked not later than turn of the century, and there wasn't a car on the lot older than 1930. But who bothers with details?

The uses of the Music Room were not entirely frivolous. Religious services of the fundamentalist Protestant variety were held there—not on Sundays, when pastors were presumably occupied with their regular flocks, but on either Tuesdays or Wednesdays. Urged on by Ann Keim and Crystal, I went twice to hear the earnest young man calling himself Brother Paul. He was a truly gentle and sincere person, one filled, or at least striving to be filled, with Christian love. (One also who, regrettably, read from a modern version of the Scriptures.) But for all of his loving kindness, he stressed the Christian doctrine that in Adam we have all sinned, and he urged us to accept Jesus Christ as our personal Saviour so that we might be spared from the wrath to come. In response, tears of repentance rolled down the beautiful African faces of Mrs. Brown and her companion. Others were less demonstrative, but more than a few seemed deeply disturbed, touched by the conviction of sin. (As if, granting the existence of a vengeful God, we all hadn't suffered enough to pay our debts!)

Brother Paul's wife played the piano. She was younger than Mrs. Delacourt's daughter-in-law, but quite as drab, and even wearier looking, since she was in a state of advanced pregnancy. Hymn books were passed out. There were never enough to go around and none ever came to me. Ann and Crystal stood near the doorway, keeping a vigilant eye upon the ever-restless congregation and singing lustily, perhaps from a sense of duty. Or, for all I know, conviction.

Brother Paul began the second meeting that I attended by

confiding in us that he had wrestled all the previous night with the Devil. Satan had come to him in the guise of sweet reason, arguing that he should forsake his mission to preach the gospel and get into some better-paying line of work, counseling or business, so that he might provide better for his family. With the dawn, conscience had prevailed and he had determined to go on doing God's work. Sighs of admiration flowed from the little assemblage. I couldn't help wondering what the outcome of his struggle might have been if he had consulted his work-worn helpmate instead of his conscience.

These gatherings were fairly well attended, filling the Music Room to capacity. After all, they furnished a break in the monotony. The black women were always there, afghans protecting their chilly old legs, hearts warm and receptive. Mr. Dole (ex-preacher, destroyer of Bibles) sat in the front row, crowded up as closely as possible to the organ. Hank would come in and get nicely settled, only to shove his way out again as the service got under way.

Another constant though even more restless attendant was a tiny little stick of a woman I knew only as Ida. She was ambulatory, under the compulsion to change her position every few minutes. Her face was without expression, her tiny pink tongue flicking in and out of her pursed lips like the tongue of a serpent, except that it was plumper and not forked. That tongue was never still for an instant except when she asked with exquisite courtesy, "May I pass?" or "May I sit here?" But she was never settled. In two or three minutes at the most she would be up and seeking a new location. Ann Keim said she was ninety-four years old. Because of the constantly darting tongue, and because she never paid the slightest attention when spoken to, I assumed she was mentally deficient. But Ann said not so; merely stone deaf. (Ida was just as restless in the dining room except when actually eating. She went into paroxysms of anxiety until her tray arrived, then consumed everything on it greedily. Sometimes a large, distinguished-looking man came and sat beside her at the table. He was her son, and rumor had it that he was a prominent professional man.)

Florence and certain other devout Catholics passed up Brother Paul, and Lura never came, although she often read aloud to herself in the evening from various religious tracts, slowly and with difficulty, pausing frequently to voice her assent to the doctrine propounded, whatever it was.

The other minister who held forth in the Music Room was of the hellfire-'n-damnation school. I don't recall if he alternated weeks with Brother Paul or if they preached on different days of the week. I never attended his services—it would be inaccurate to say I never heard him, since it would have been impossible not to have heard him. Fortunately his voice reached Room 36 only as a blurred shouting. I was in no mood even to be mildly amused by threats of the wrath to come; a hypothetical hell interested me less than the stubbornly persistent hope of escaping from a present Limbo. But I can imagine the pangs of guilt and fear which shook many a failing heart at his assaults. (My mother, through most of her life, enjoyed hellfire-'n-damnation sermons—and no wonder, for she loved to read about eruptions, hurricanes, and all violent and destructive natural phenomena; but in her last illness she lifted a feeble hand and turned off her radio when the preacher embarked on such a theme. To opt for blessed silence was almost her last voluntary act.)

The spiritual needs of Catholic patients were not neglected. In addition to the ministrations of Deacon North, Mass was said on the third Saturday of each month. When the third Saturday of September came around, Florence and Mike invited me to attend with them. I said that I would love to do so, but I felt a certain timidity because I was not a Catholic. They assured me that many patients attended who were not Catholic. Thereafter I really looked forward to the experience.

During the course of my whole life, even when I called myself an atheist, I have felt strangely drawn to the ancient rituals of the Catholic Church; never to very much of its dogma and only minimally and occasionally to its discipline, but feeling mightily the pull of its mysterious and colorful rites. Perhaps if I had been brought up in the Church of Rome its mysteries would have seemed less mysterious and therefore less attractive. The very fact that in my childhood Catholicism was the religion of Antichrist, embodying all that was wicked and forbidden, helped to strengthen the pull. As a very small child I stood beside my mother in the Methodist church and listened carefully when she recited the Apostle's Creed. Even then, along with a certain confusion and fear, I remember another emotion, a kind of fearful secret joy, when she uttered the words, "I believe in the Holy Catholic Church." For as long as I can remember, I tried to reason things out, to wrestle with things beyond my understanding; only now, in my advanced old age, have I learned quietly and even joyously to accept the fact that the universe is inexplicable. The confused little creature, barely past infancy, sheltering in her mother's skirts, tried hard to understand: "Catholics are bad. But they are not all bad people, because Mrs. (Whatever her name was) is Catholic and Mama likes her. Jews are bad, But Mr. and Mrs. Litt are Jews and we like them, we go to their store all the time. Mama said 'Holy Catholic Church.' Maybe we are all Catholics, but we don't say it except on Sunday."

Shortly after we moved to San Diego in 1913, I bought myself a prayerbook and a rosary; and twice, braving my mother's tight-lipped disapproval, I attended Mass at St. Joseph's, sitting ill at ease and self-conscious in one of the rear pews. Years later, when I wasn't too sleepy on Christmas Eve, I watched Midnight Mass on the television; but much of the charm went out of it when English was substituted for Latin.

Now I was about to hear Mass at Golden Mesa. Mike took Florence and promised to return for me. But in a few minutes he wheeled her back into the room. They had met people in the corridor who had told them Father Murray couldn't come. He'd sent word at the last minute—some kind of conflicting engagement. Florence said if he had known how disappointed the patients in Golden Mesa would be, he surely would have made other arrangements.

Time dragged on in its peculiarly timeless way, which can certainly be understood only by those who have been confined in nursing homes or prisons. On the third Saturday of October there was no question but what I would go with Florence. Mike had appeared the day before with a severe cold, and Florence had strictly enjoined him to stay at home and rest in bed. Visitors willingly wheeled us both into the dining room, now transformed into a place of worship.

A table had been spread with a white cloth. Father Murray and Deacon North put on thin white garments, through which their black suits were clearly visible. There was a woman, referred to as "Sister Mildred," wearing a really beautiful pink jumper over a long-sleeved blouse with a floral pattern in pink, green, and purple. I thought she must be some kind of a lay sister, but Florence told me later that she was a nun in secular dress. It seemed to me a very thoughtful gesture to wear something so gay to Golden Mesa.

The persons attending included many of those whom I had seen at Protestant services. The black women weren't there, nor Hank, and I don't remember Ida, with her restless feet and flickering tongue. But Mr. Dole's wheelchair was as close as possible to the improvised altar. And there were others whom I had not seen before; notably one tiny little woman in a wheelchair, clutching a rosary in her hand. Her face reminded me of one of my first dolls, the one with china head, hands, and feet sewn onto a flexible kid body. The doll's feet were painted to look like black high-topped buttoned shoes. The face and hands were dead white, with a red mouth and blue eyes painted on the face, and black hair on the head. The little lady in the wheelchair had white hair, but her face was as white, unwrinkled, and expressionless as my doll's had been. Her tiny rosebud mouth might have been painted on; and the hands holding the rosary were as white and almost as immobile as if they had been made of china. She sat very still, very erect in her wheelchair. I think she wore a white shawl. The whole effect was something of a cross between a small, preternaturally well-behaved child and a large old-fashioned doll. I learned afterwards that she was one hundred and three years old.

Father Murray began informally, striking his breast lightly in the immemorial gesture of contrition and saying "mea culpa." He had no excuses, he said. He had simply forgotten that it was the third Saturday of the month until it was too late to change his arrangements. He would try never to let it happen again. I don't remember what else he said, except that his sermon was brief and ecumenical, calculated neither to tire nor to offend the mixed bag of his congregation.

The moment came for partaking of the Sacrament. Florence and I were seated in about the middle of the front row, with the little china doll at our far right, and Mr. Dole a little to her right and slightly in front. Father Murray and Deacon North approached from our left. I noticed that he offered the Sacrament to everyone, and I assumed that he thought all present were Catholics and were in a proper state of grace. (I believe the announcement had been made earlier that he was available to hear confessions.)

For some reason I wanted to partake of the Sacrament, but I knew of course I could not. When he offered it to me, I drew back and said, "Father, I am not a Catholic."

I don't remember his exact response—something to the effect that "we don't go as much by labels as we used to." Then he asked, "Do you believe that the Lord is present?"

"With all my heart!" I answered. Then he laid the wafer on my tongue.

Priest and Deacon passed along the front row of wheelchairs, administering the Sacrament to each person. In their smooth progression they reached Mr. Dole. All was quiet, all was reverential, there was no hint of discord or disrespect. Mr. Dole received the Host—and spat out a particle upon the altar cloth! Sister Mildred and Deacon North winced visibly; and I caught—or imagined that I caught—a shadow of pure horror on Father Murray's face. Nothing was said. At the close of the ceremony, Father Murray requested that each of us shake our neighbor's hand as a gesture of love and friendship. Florence and I turned to each other spontaneously. I took her poor, distorted hand and she exerted as much pressure as she could in return. We truly loved each other, and now that love was cemented.

Sister Mildred carefully brushed the altar cloth so that no crumb of consecrated bread might be shaken off onto the floor. I am not familiar enough with Catholic ritual to know if that is standard procedure.

What prompted Mr. Dole's rejection of the body of Christ? Did he simply not like the taste of the wafer? Probably. I do not believe his brain functioned consistently enough to enable him to be guilty of a reasoned act of sacrilege. But remember that he, a man who never missed a religious service, Catholic or Protestant, was also the man who had mutilated all the Bibles in the library at Golden Mesa. He appeared to have a curious love/hate relationship to religion. Perhaps he felt that God had let him down, and subconsciously he wanted revenge.

The cold that prevented Mike from attending Mass that third Saturday in October had probably been contracted at Golden Mesa. An epidemic of severe colds or flu had swept through the institution, afflicting patients and attendants alike. It was for this that the Kramers' personal physician had been summoned. Florence had had pneumonia the previous winter, and only the vigilant Dragon Lady had detected her condition in time for successful treatment. This time the respiratory trouble was less severe, but her devoted family took no chances. I am quite certain that several patients passed on during this epidemic, but naturally we were not informed. (Way back in September—what? Only a month ago?—Willie Mike had died of despair, diagnosed as pneumonia; but that had no connection with the present epidemic.)

Almost every day several of the aides with high fevers and running noses breathed into my face as they gave me my "evening care." Golden Mesa was now more shorthanded than ever; and no effort was made to stop any "girl" who was willing and able—sometimes barely able—to keep on her feet from coming into close contact with frail and elderly patients. Only I, who throughout most of my life had considered myself to be "cold susceptible," did not contract even a scratchy throat or a sniffle.

The Vitamin C which I had persuaded Dr. Bertman to give me in the belief that it would help my sore gums was still available and I continued to take it. Considering our miserable diet, a vitamin supplement could surely do no harm. Only on one occasion did I refuse it. One night when I was unable to sleep, climbing the walls with nervousness (or would have been, had I been able to get out of bed unaided and stand upon my feet), a nurse soothingly offered "something to quiet your nerves." Before I could swallow the white tablet, I recognized the taste of ascorbic acid. I took it out of my mouth and remarked with some bitterness, "What are you trying to do? Conduct a negavitamin experiment? I've already had 500 milligrams of this today." But this dosage may have contributed to my immunity. Perhaps I am a walking (?) advertisement of the efficacy of Vitamin C.

Or perhaps not. Gradually and fitfully I was getting command of my thoughts. Reason told me I was no less a part of the on-going Life of the universe because I had partaken of the body of Christ in the ancient sacrifice of the Mass. Something more primitive and powerful than reason told me differently. My mystical sense of union was definitely strengthened by participation in a rite whose power had been reenforced by the belief of millions of persons through nearly twenty centuries.

The only Psalm I could remember in its entirety was the 23rd (according to the King James Version). I said it over and over, silently, till—had I been using a material object—I would have almost worn it out. "And I will dwell in the house of the Lord forever." I had told Father Murray that I believed with all my heart in the Lord's presence. Then would not consistency demand that Golden Mesa was the house of the Lord? But I felt more and more strongly that for me "the house of the Lord" would be quite different. "In my Father's house are many mansions. I go to prepare a place for you." Those lines I remember from the New Testament, and for me they constituted a promise of new hope on earth, not of Paradise after death; which, in spite of my age and infirmity, concerned me very little.

7

On two occasions during my stay in Golden Mesa I began to keep a diary. The first was immediately after the "Watermelon Bust." The second, perhaps a week later. Neither time did I write more than four or five lines on a ruled writing tablet. I can't explain even to myself why I never persisted—why I was unable to persist—in the effort. I felt an inner certainty that, if I ever escaped from that place, or perhaps even if I didn't, I would one day write about it. My primary reason, however, for wanting some record of the days was purely and simply a matter of orientation, of affirming my own existence in the world; at the very least in that microcosm in which I found myself, thereby maintaining a tenuous relationship to the world of reality. But I found (perhaps from sheer discouragement or from my own fuzzy mental condition, or from a combination of inward and outward pressures) that I could not keep a record, although I had no difficulty in writing letters. Letter writing was my great pleasure, especially as my contacts gradually increased.

I wish now that I had succeeded with the diary, for it would enable me to date accurately and to place in proper perspective the first great breakthrough to life outside the walls of Golden Mesa.

One evening after I had been tucked in for the night—lying

in bed with no thought except the hope that my evening reading would be interesting, that I would sleep soundly and my arms wouldn't cramp too severely, and that Lura would keep reasonably quiet—a nurse came hurrying in in a state of some excitement. I must get up and into a wheelchair at once, I had to come to the telephone, it was important, it was *long distance* (My God, hadn't I been trying to make a long-distance call ever since I arrived!) and the party was waiting. . . .

I knew Harry Lawton mainly as the Chairman of the Editorial Board of Malki Museum Press, a unique undertaking involving both Indians and non-Indians. But that is only one of his activities. He is a man of tremendous talent, inexhaustible energy, and many parts. I believe his official position is Administrative Analyst at University of California, Riverside. But that doesn't begin to tell the story. He is a notable author. He teaches (or was teaching at that time) classes in creative writing at the University. He founded *The Journal of California Anthropology*. I first met him in May of 1971 at the annual Malki Fiesta on Morongo Indian Reservation, near Banning, California. This was after Professor Lowell Bean of California State University, Hayward, had, quite accidentally, discovered that I had written a manuscript entitled *The Chemehuevis*, a fairly complete ethnological and ethnographic account of a small tribe about which virtually nothing was known.

Harry had been told by the authorities at Golden Mesa that I could not be disturbed and that only relatives were permitted to speak with patients. He had bludgeoned his way through by saying that unless he was allowed to speak to me, he would phone the head of the Bureau of Indian Affairs in Washington, D.C. Now his voice came over the wire, strong, enthusiastic, reassuringly—almost incredibly—real. I don't remember how I reacted. I hope it was with some degree of composure; but if I did not weep, that was a true miracle. Harry said that the galley proofs of *Encounter with an Angry God* were now ready for me to proofread and that he was forwarding them immediately.

Back in my bed, one thing stood out clearly: I really was

a woman who had written two books, both of which were actually in press. I was not an elderly patient in a nursing home who fantasized that she had written two books and that they had been accepted for publication. Not that I had actually come to the point of doubting my true identity, except occasionally in the long, confused nights, when I drifted between sleep and waking. This particular night I did not care whether I slept at all. My mind at last was fully awake. The temptation presented itself briefly to doubt whether I was capable of the work before me, but by this time I knew enough about publishing to know that if I missed something someone else would find it; and I could already think of a few places which I could clarify with a word or two.

The first parcel—the first four chapters, I believe—arrived two or three days later. The fat manila envelope was addressed to "Professor Carobeth Laird." During my stay at Golden Mesa Harry never sent me anything without putting "Professor" or "Dr." before my name. He understood human nature well enough to know the effect of a degree, however informally bestowed.

Dorothy Williams had been unfailingly kind to me. Now she volunteered the use of her office. This, I found, consisted of a smallish desk crammed into a corner of the Therapy Room, which was otherwise filled with various types of equipment. I said I thought it was a shame that both she and the social worker should have such makeshift offices. But she was not to be drawn into complaint or criticism; she said she really had such a small amount of paperwork that this desk served her purpose very well.

I began work immediately. I believe someone carried the galley proofs for me, and at times I was assisted in wheeling myself. Already a more gracious atmosphere was beginning to envelope me. I was beginning to experience that vast respect America has for the printed word, even though only in galley proof.

The second or third day that I worked in Dorothy's office, a man appeared in the door and exclaimed in horror, "You don't belong in here. You have to get out right away!"

"Mrs. Williams has given me permission to use her desk," I explained.

"No! Dorothy's assigned me to watch this place, and nobody comes in."

I went on correcting proof, and after a while he went away. When I told Dorothy about it, she said, "Yes, that's Maurice. I'll explain things to him."

Maurice had been the principal resident celebrity—until it became generally known that I actually had written a book which was shortly going to be published. Then he had to share the glory. He had been a musician, and now that he was no longer able to perform, had taken up painting. His paintings were held in high esteem at Golden Mesa, and some of them were raffled off at twenty-five cents a chance. I got a glimpse of an unfinished one that he once brought into the dining room. It was a landscape—all shades of green with trees and a stream. I was glad he had the courage not to choose autumnal colors.

I am quite sure Maurice was the man I had overheard holding forth on the subject of the splendid job his daughter (or sister?) had obtained for him in San Francisco, a job which would be open in the spring. When I heard this remark, on one of my rare visits to the TV Room, I classified it as a daydream based on wishful thinking. Now I truly hope that his prospective job proved as substantial as the publication of my books.

I also remember Maurice as the owner of the walker the institution loaned me during my stay in Golden Mesa. It seems to me that he was ambulatory at the time he attempted to drive me away from Dorothy's desk in the Therapy Room. Or possibly he had regressed to a wheelchair. I saw so many people in wheelchairs that I tend to remember everyone in that way.

The Kramers were heartily glad for me. I think that they and the Haases, mother and daughter, were probably the only ones who had not doubted the existence of my books.

For the Kramers, too, change was in the air. It was apparent that Florence had profited all that she could from the therapy available at Golden Mesa. Although she still could not rise to

a standing position without aid, she could walk with her walker, or even without it, leaning on Mike's arm, for what seemed
to me incredible distances. She had walked to the Hobby
Room and clear out to the patio and even, on one occasion,
to the kitchen. (Florence had a very warm feeling for the
cook. She said that for a time after she first arrived he had
prepared little individual tarts for dessert and a number of
other delectable dishes. But for many months now, under the
combined pressure of rising prices and rising cupidity, the
cuisine had steadily deteriorated.) Now that she was as well
as she was ever likely to be and increasingly active, there
seemed to be no reason why she should not go home. "Home"
would not be the home she and Mike had lived in before her
various illnesses. That was long since sold. Since Mike had decided he preferred lonely independence to the loving hospital-
ity of Jeanette and her husband, he had been living in a doubtless dreary though highly functional "utility apartment."
Now he planned to move into something more pleasant and
spacious, ground floor, of course, and with a pool that Florence could sit beside in her wheelchair. He was already performing many small services for her. No doubt he could manage nicely, with Jeanette coming in one day a week and the
help, if needed, of a visiting nurse.

I knew that I would miss Florence sorely, but it was not in
my heart to begrudge anyone the blessed privilege of going
home. With the selfishness of age, however, I determined
to derive all possible advantage from the change. I asked
a nurse, "When Mrs. Kramer leaves, may I have her bed by
the window?"

"Why certainly, I don't see why not," was the prompt and
gracious response.

Before parcels and letters began arriving for "Professor
Laird," I am sure the reaction would have been quite different. Now when I said that I sorely missed my typewriter,
I was assured that if I could have it sent over from my daughter's home it could occupy the corner now filled by Mrs.
Kramer's electric armchair. There would be no difficulty at
all about locating a sturdy table for it.

I wish I could remember the name of the nurse who was so agreeable about my change of beds and the possibility of accomodating my typewriter. She was the one with whom I felt the most at ease and she certainly never showed me anything but kindness, although she played no favorites. I, too, made it a rule to show courtesy to nurses, nurses' aides, and housekeepers; even the occasional contests of wills did not degenerate into shouting matches. Yet when I slipped into making something like a threat, it was directed towards this woman, surely the one who least deserved it.

She encountered me in the corridor one day as I laboriously propelled myself back to my room from the dining room. Pausing to chat (this, remember, was after my change in status), she remarked brightly, yet with what seemed to me like a faint undercurrent of anxiety, "Now I suppose you'll be writing a book about us?"

A diabolical impulse took over—such impulses not infrequently assail those who set themselves up to live by the Beatitudes and/or the Noble Eight-fold Path—and I replied through clenched teeth, "And what a book!"

The cold which prevented Mike from attending Mass on the third Saturday of October was not lasting nor severe enough to interfere with the Kramer's plans. It was very shortly after that service that Florence left—perhaps it was the imminence of separation which had heightened our emotions when we clasped hands. There was a flurry of packing; goodbyes from all the people to whom she had endeared herself; a final shower, although it wasn't the day on which the occupants of Room 36 were scheduled to have showers; Mike arriving; Jeanette and Durbin arriving to assist with the move—and then, our final, hasty good-bye. Happy as she was to go home, I think she was sorry to part from me, and even the prospect of a bed by the window could not compensate me for the loss of such a companion. I suppose we both knew we would not meet again.

Florence's bed was scrubbed as regulations demanded, the linen was changed, and soon I was ensconced in it. My letter-

writing materials and—most important—my galley proofs
were transferred to the drawer where Florence had kept her
rosary and religious pamphlets. Dorothy had insisted that my
proofs be brought back each evening when I finished work
and kept in my bedside table. I didn't see why they wouldn't
be equally safe on her desk; but she said that she could not
assume responsibility. Although no one would intentionally
damage my proofs, some of the patients might handle them
and unintentionally mess them up. This oblique reference to
the simian curiosity and destructiveness of the senile was the
closest Dorothy ever came to a derogatory remark.

The difference in perspective which a change of beds made
was enormous. I had asked for the change principally because
I wanted to put a little more space between myself and Lura.
I thought I could sleep better if her nighttime monologues
were less audible; also it would be a relief to be free of her
comments on my evening reading, on whether or not my curtains were partially drawn, and on my water-drinking habits—
Lura thought it disgusting that I should sip water from a glass
which had been standing uncovered, I thought it disgusting
that she should sleep with her bedpan; she voiced her opinion
audibly and frequently, I kept mine to myself. In the bed next
to the window it did indeed come about that I was relieved
of these petty annoyances, but this relief was scarcely noticed
in my joy at attaining a new view of the outdoors.

I could see the redwood fence, partially discolored by water,
which Florence had remarked upon—she had spoken frequently of the effect of water upon redwood in this climate, and
I had agreed without the faintest notion of what she was talking about. This fence, I now perceived, joined the low stuc-
coed wall at the far end of the grounds. I could watch Joe
pruning the shrubs next to the building. I could see into the
ditch which paralleled the road (a ditch the presence of which
I had previously deduced from the way that dogs running
along the road would suddenly drop from sight and from the
tops of the tall, straggly weeds growing in it). I could even,
when I sat up in bed, see the front door of Lura's long, gray

"nut-house," and the people who went in and out with bags of groceries. I think at least some of the dwellers in that house had been away on a long summer vacation and were now busily putting things in order for winter. A man came out now and then to prune trees and shrubbery. Four or five women, mostly young, and another man or two walked about in the roomy backyard and there was much airing of quilts and blankets on the long clothesline. (The front door was out of Lura's range of vision. I am sure she could have seen the activity at sides and rear of the house if she had cared to, but she closed her mind to it. These things did not jibe with her theory of a house whose crazy or criminal inmates were forever confined to dark and airless rooms although supervised by the sun-loving "little old man" who lived on the roof.)

I could now see that the heavily wooded canal—it must indeed have been a very old canal—slanted away at an obtuse angle to the roadway, and I could locate that particular tree ("shaped just like a Christmas tree") which Florence had so much admired. The shades of green were lush and pleasant in that desert land. But curiously—considering my deep revulsion for the autumnal paintings in Golden Mesa—the object that gave me the most pleasure was a medium-sized deciduous tree. Apparently there was only one such tree along all that stretch of waterway. Now, in early autumn, it was bare of leaves. When the morning "girl" opened the drapes shortly before sunrise I could watch the growing light turn its delicate tracery of bare brown branches to rosy gold; and the same transformation took place towards sunset, except that then the color was deeper, verging on copper. To gaze at this tree in its semitropical setting at all hours and in all lights, never twice quite the same, afforded me the most exquisite pleasure that I experienced in all that drab period.

Morning and evening joggers went up and down the dusty road; sometimes dogs that were being taken for a walk—big, beautiful dogs—ran free and explored the ditch; horseback riders cantered back and forth; groups of children and teenagers passed by, chattering and shoving at each other; and always there were the tall green trees and the especial magic of the little tree that had no leaves. From the vantage point of the bed by the window I felt much closer to the world of ongoing life, the world which held other things besides age and mental aberration and preoccupation with dreary physical routines.

One morning as I ate my unappetizing breakfast and gazed out the window, a morning "girl," anxious to get on with her work, snatched my tray.

"Hey! Bring that back!" I said, "I'm not nearly through eating."

"You were looking out the window," she replied. Her tone was both injured and accusatory. Suddenly I was horribly depressed. Obviously I belonged to that category of persons under authority—patients/inmates/prisoners—who must perform their necessary functions in the time assigned, without dawdling.

Florence had left before the Halloween Party. She might have attended had she still been there, for I know she did not find these "entertainments" as ghastly as they seemed to me. The preceding Valentine's Day she attended the party (Mike, of course, had been with her) and had been unanimously voted the "Sweetheart of Golden Mesa." For at least a month the staff had been whipping up expectations of this Halloween Party. When the night came, I flatly refused to go. I preferred a peaceful evening reading—although I was beginning to be dissatisfied with the paucity of my mental fare. (I was still borrowing Reader's Digest Condensed Books from Ann Keim and gothic novels from Becky. Pamela Munro had sent me a paper on linguistics, but that was too technical for me—the person who trained me had had his own peculiar system, which did not include such terms as phoneme or morpheme. The galley proofs were too awkward to work on in bed, and anyway I couldn't reach into the drawer where they were kept.)

When the night of All Saints' Day came around, I asked one of the evening aides, "How did the party go?"

"Terrible," she responded. Pressed for details, she said a number of the old people had been violently sick to their stomachs, and I was also left with the impression that there had been some quarreling. I wondered if certain ones had not perhaps regressed so far back into individual and racial childhood that they found the images of witches, goblins, and black cats genuinely terrifying; or perhaps they had merely suffered from staying up past their accustomed bedtimes, eating too late, being costumed more or less against their will. Surely they must all have been fatigued and querulous, and latent antagonisms must have been exacerbated. But what difference could all that make to those concerned with the image of the institution? The Halloween posters came down, the Thanksgiving posters went up, and all energies were directed towards the appearance of giving the tenderly cherished patients a happy and homelike Thanksgiving Day. Families need feel no compulsion to try to take Grandpa or Mother or Aunt Jane home for Thanksgiving.

There was, however, an outing in which I did participate. The women of St. Thomas Parish invited the residents in all nursing and convalescents homes in and near Phoenix to a luncheon which would be preceded by a special Mass for the sick. Transportation would be provided; wheelchairs would pose no problem. I found myself eager to go, with very little of the timidity that had influenced my refusal to go with the young Mormons.

On the appointed morning my wheelchair was pushed up a ramp (or hoisted—I forget the precise technique) into a van. I was taken up first, and after me came Señora Moreno's roommate, wringing her hands and uttering piteous cries in Spanish. It seems that she had an intense fear of falling. Although our chairs were carefully wedged in place to prevent their slipping forward or backward, and although the driver proceeded with the utmost caution, the trip was a nightmare to her. I enjoyed it, although I rather resented not having been transported by car so that I might have had a better view of the city. But when we reached our destination, I saw that I could never have managed without the wheelchair.

The church (cathedral? I must repeat that I am abysmally ignorant of such matters) was imposing. Light filtered through stained-glass windows into an interior dim enough to be appropriately mysterious without giving the impression of gloom. It was evident that this Mass would have all the trappings so notably absent in the service conducted by Father Murray at Golden Mesa, but I doubted if it could move me any more deeply. I found myself propelled to a central position in front of the first row of pews. A little to one side of me were two young men in what appeared to be oversized cribs. I have never seen more piteous individuals in my whole life. They must have been victims of the same type of brain damage which afflicted Mary Mitchell's little granddaughter. Their normal heads appeared oversized in comparison with the underdeveloped bodies and useless, stick-like arms and legs. I do not know if they could speak, or if so, how intelligibly; but both faces unmistakably registered awareness of their surroundings and of their condition. Contemplating them with awful fascination, I realized how unforgivable was my own desire to be cared for, to have no responsibilities and no anxieties. These youths, who should have been enjoying the full vigor of their young manhood, would be cared for, fed and clothed, every day of their lives; they would be without anxiety—and without hope.

All the deaf had obviously been grouped together to the left of the rest of the congregation. Before them stood two men dressed in black who translated the service into sign language. Coincidentally perhaps, the lay reader was himself disabled, dragging himself with difficulty to a small podium, and kneeling with even more difficulty; this was, after all, a Mass for the lame, the halt, and the blind—not to mention the senile and the deaf.

Was the service conducted by a bishop? I seem to remember a mitre, but perhaps I am confusing this mass with Christmas Masses that I have viewed on television. I remember distinctly the green vestments, the bright red robes of the altar boys. These, together with the dim light, the high, stained-glass windows, and the music provided a pleasant atmosphere of solemnity and mystery, compensating somewhat for Mass said in the vernacular. Some persons in the pew behind me, Catholics from birth no doubt, so familiar with the service that they found if commonplace, kept up an intermittent flow of whispered gossip. I felt appropriately indignant.

This sermon impressed itself upon me more than Father Murray's. I particularly recall the statement that we were not to expect justice from God. It may have been qualified by some such phrase as "in this life" or "in human experience." Of that I am uncertain; but I can never forget the stark words: "God is not just." At times when I formulated my thoughts in a religious context, I had always thought of justice as an attribute of God: "Justice and judgment are the habitation of thy throne." Now, looking at the pitiful travesties of young manhood lying in their cradles before me, afflicted from infancy, I was forced to admit that, given the premise of an omnipotent and omniscient Deity, for them there was no justice. Unless, that is, we were all under the law of karma; and even that seemed horribly unjust—why should one suffer for sins, deviations, errors he did not even remember? I did not hear or did not remember anymore of the sermon.

Printed sheets were passed among the congregation, so that all might join in the hymns. One of them was "Amazing Grace," which always, with a power beyond logic, lifts my heart. The last time I had heard it was on some televised evangelical service. The soloist had looked like a broken-down prizefighter, a refugee from skid row, and he had had a perfectly glorious voice. I listened to him, then turned off the screeching preacher.

I wondered if, in this more formal setting, I would be al-

lowed to receive the Sacrament. Again I made my honest dis-
claimer, "Father, I am not a Catholic." This time the question
asked in return came a little more sharply: "You have been
baptized, haven't you?" "Yes," I replied, with mingled senti-
ments of gratitude to my parents for having had the rite of
infant baptism performed in the Methodist church, and disappointment, because the condition laid down was ritualistic.
After the Sacrament came the anointing with oil, the sign of the
cross upon my forehead, and a kiss of fellowship on my cheek.

(A washcloth was not part of the evening care at Golden
Mesa. In the night, still feeling the holy oil upon my unwashed
forehead, I found myself recalling once-familiar words: "Is
any sick among you? Let him call for the elders of the church;
and let them pray over him, anointing him with oil in the
name of the Lord. . . . The effectual, fervent prayer of a right-
eous man availeth much." Who was I to deny that efficacy?
Wiser ones than I had believed in it.)

The feast for the body came after the feast for the soul.
Tables had been pushed together to form one long table, seating close to two hundred persons. The luncheon fare was simple, nothing fancy to upset frail or aged stomachs. Actually
the menu might have been a Golden Mesa menu—but what
a difference in quality! First came a plain jello salad, then
roast beef with mashed potatoes and gravy and green beans,
followed by a small piece of plain cake for dessert. The roast
beef was delicious, real meat, no wondering about what sort
of animal it might have come from; the mashed potatoes had
been peeled and cooked and whipped with butter and milk;
the brown gravy had been made from the rich caramel in the
roasting pan; the green beans were fresh green beans, well
cooked and seasoned. And all through the meal the young
people from the parish school for the educable retarded kept
passing baskets of soft, fresh rolls, kept hot under immaculate
napkins, and refilling our cups with delicious, fresh-made,
scalding hot coffee. The boys and girls who served us glowed
with happy self-importance. They were so eager to do everything correctly. "Normal" youngsters might have been a little

bored, more than a little contemptuous of the physically impaired or the senile. Only in relaxation did these retarded
ones seem younger than their ages. One girl who appeared to
be about sixteen had buck teeth and a perpetual smile. After
the luncheon was over she amused herself by scooting about
in a vacant wheelchair.

This whole experience was a memorable one for me. But
my critical faculty was beginning to awaken. I noted that
among the kind women of the parish there was not one black
person, not one Chicano or Native American. There were, in
fact, only two dark faces: a Hindu woman, wearing gold
hoops in her ears and a filmy blue sari, and her small daughter.
The ladies of the parish were very attentive to them.

Shortly before Florence's departure a tragic change had
taken place in Room 35, the room directly across the corridor. The woman in her eighties who had been a frequent visitor in our room, the one whose strength and ability in using
her walker I had so envied in spite of her confession that she
took each step with fear, got up in the night, as was her cus-
tom, to use the bathroom. She fell and fractured her hip.
Whether she fainted and was unable to call out, or whether
Miss Anderson and the occupants of the room failed to hear
her and summon help, I do not know. But I understand that
she lay for a time unattended. She was removed to a hospital.
We asked when she would be coming back—after all, Mrs.
Haase was in Golden Mesa to recuperate from a broken hip—
but it seemed that this particular patient was not likely to return. So now it was coming about that Miss May Anderson
was losing the only roommate with whom she felt some degree of congeniality, just as I—just as both of us—had lost
Florence.

The center bed in Room 35 did not remain empty more
than a couple of days, if that long. I presume Golden Mesa
had a waiting list, since it was rated as one of the better places
within its price range—six hundred dollars per month. I asked
once what the total population was, and was informed that at

the moment there were one hundred and ten. Probably this was near the total capacity.

The new occupant was about Annie's age or a little younger. In a way, her situation was even more tragic. Annie had always been retarded. In her no vestiges of normalcy struggled for resurrection. This woman, on the other hand, had been a happy wife and mother. I had a fairly good look at her once or twice. Even in a wheelchair, it was apparent that she was a tall slender woman. She had dark eyes, lovely features, a smooth, olive complexion—without that vacant, harried expression, she would have been beautiful. A nurse told me she "had Indian blood" (that is, in these days, more than acceptable in the prosperous and socially well-placed—it even adds a touch of glamor). This woman's condition was the result of oxygen deprivation occurring during open-heart surgery. The surgery, I believe, had been reasonably successful; the mind was gone forever.

She could speak. In fact, during the first few days she spoke constantly in a loud, hoarse voice, articulating her words with great difficulty. Her husband came to see her, but did not attempt to bring their two young children. Tall and elegant young women came; I think they were her sisters. I don't know if she recognized them or if anything that she said to them made sense. She had delusions, and was subject to fits of anger. One evening she threatened May Anderson, because she said that May was occupying her bed. For the first two nights her voice went on continually in those harsh, painfully articulated, incoherent protests. Even across the hall, sleep was out of the question. The nurse I spoke to said sedation had no effect; the new patient was "having some trouble adjusting." "Adjusting" and "adjustment" were words much in use by the staff at Golden Mesa. Patients were always perfectly happy once they had "made a proper adjustment."

The middle bed in Room 36, the bed I had lately vacated, was also filled quite promptly. Mrs. Chancellor had been in Golden Mesa for some days, sharing a room with the two

deaf ladies and their television. But she was desperately unhappy there, and it was thought she might "adjust more rap-
idly" in a quieter environment. My old bed was rolled out
and Mrs. Chancellor's was brought in. I noticed that it was
a few inches lower than the bed I was occupying. "If I had
a bed that low, if one of the sides was left down and my
walker within reach, I could go to the bathroom unassisted
at night," I said, explaining that it was only because my legs
were so short that I couldn't get back in my own hospital bed,
although I could get myself out of it quite well. "Why the
difference in height?" I asked. "Not all the beds were manufactured by the same company." "And why couldn't a lower
bed be brought in for me?" I was informed vaguely that that
wasn't hospital practice. Anyway, I'd tried. All my desire to
be more active, to do as much for myself as possible, had
now returned.

Mrs. Chancellor had been for many years a busy and successful chiropractor. In Hilda's case nothing remained except
the desire to supervise and dominate; with Mrs. Chancellor it
was the desire to be active and to serve.

She was ambulatory, and restless beyond belief. A large
woman, with hunched shoulders and painfully swollen feet
and ankles, she was supposed to walk leaning upon a cane.
But usually she merely dragged the cane. When she saw a patient struggling to propel himself in a wheelchair, she immediately took it upon herself to push him. Since she had a severe heart condition and was not supposed to overexert
herself, I found it extremely embarrassing to be the recipient
of her kindness. The first time this occurred was at dinner-
time. She did not know—did not remember from one day to
the next—where the dining room was. I said, "Walk along
with me and I'll show you." (Even before Florence left, I had
for some time been required to make the daily pilgrimage;
theoretically it was for my own good that I was no longer
allowed the indulgence of a tray in my room, actually I'm
sure the purpose was to bolster the institutional image—"we
keep all our patients active.") We started out with Mrs. Chan-

cellor walking beside my chair. Within a few yards she had
taken over. We met a nurse who rebuked us both severely,
but no sooner had she gone on her way than Mrs. Chancellor
was pushing me again.

Her conversation seemed, at first impression, to be coherent. But there was very little memory, none at all of recent
events. Half an hour after we returned from the dining room,
she asked me, "Have we eaten yet?" She told me that she was
seventy-two years old and that she had sold her house just before "coming here." One of her daughters informed me that
her mother was eighty-two and had sold her house fifteen
years ago.

Mrs. Chancellor had three devoted daughters, all with
standing in their various communities—only one, I believe,
lived in Phoenix. One had a husband running for public office,
another had a daughter of her own and grandchildren, who
were sometimes brought to visit their great-grandmother. In
spite of my own prejudices in such matters, I cannot fault
them in any way for placing their mother in a nursing home.
Once, because she was so desperately restless and unhappy,
a daughter took her home over the weekend; but there she
was just as restless and unhappy, requiring ceaseless watching
and unresponsive to any efforts made on her behalf. . . . For
years I have observed this restlessness in the senile, this constant desire to go home, and the failure to feel at home in any
circumstances. Is the home they desire the half-remembered
home of mental competency and mastery over their own lives?
Is it the happy home of childhood? Or is it the house of death
itself, the final home that waits for all of us?

Mrs. Chancellor's daughters brought her fruit, grapes and
melons, to supplement the institutional fare, and they always
brought enough for the other occupants of Room 36. When,
responding to their inquiry, I said we had not been served
any melons lately, they went to the kitchen and found seven
untouched honeydews. Thereafter we had melon daily, which
Mrs. Chancellor perversely refused to touch. She didn't care
much for the grapes, either; and on the rare occasions when

grapefruit juice appeared on our breakfast trays she wanted to give it to someone else.

She was not an easy patient to care for. As mentioned, in the current parlance "she was having trouble adjusting." Although capable of visiting the bathroom by herself, she was occasionally incontinent. Her beautiful bright cloth house slippers (of which she had several pairs) squashed little piles of fecal matter and her slips sometimes had dark brown stains. She constantly "tore up" her nicely made bed, lying on top of the not-so-washable pink spread or pulling the covers down every which way. Both morning and afternoon aides were helplessly infuriated and frustrated, but there was nothing they could do. At least one of the daughters visited daily. A less-watched-over patient would have been strapped in a wheelchair, and that would have been the end of it; but orders had evidently come down from above that such measures were not to be applied to Mrs. Chancellor.

The evening aides were equally frustrated. Mrs. Chancellor would not allow herself to be put to bed. She took off her own dress, but refused to exchange her slip for a nightgown or to be tucked under the covers. At night she did not go out into the corridor but prowled around her bed for a long time, at last falling asleep on top of the covers. Nurses who came in said, "This won't do, dear. You'll take cold." Sometimes she permitted them to draw sheet and blanket over her, but as soon as she was left alone, she pushed them down.

One daughter brought Mrs. Chancellor a little hand loom and a supply of bright wool, but she could not be interested in any kind of handicraft. Only one thing really occupied her attention: the keeping track of days. Each morning she brought me a large calendar and a pencil. Each day I explained to her, "Look, this is Tuesday, the such-and-such of October. See, yesterday was Monday, we already marked it off." Then she would put a large cross on the indicated date, and with a sigh of satisfaction, return the calendar to her nightstand. When she first arrived, she attempted on one or two occasions to approach Lura with the calendar, but never obtained a coherent response. So for this small but so-important service, she came to rely on me, bringing the calendar to me early in the morning, before I had been got up for the day. She seemed to derive great satisfaction from the distinct and rather loud repetition, three or four times perhaps, of the name of the day and the date. Perhaps it was her own personal link to reality. God knows we all needed to find such a link and cling to it; those who did not were lost. My links were letters from the outside world, books, and the galley proofs. Without them I would soon have been hopelessly senile—or, like Willie Mike, safely dead.

8

My improved mental attitude was not due altogether to the tangible evidence of identity furnished by the galley proofs, to a growing correspondence, or to the spiritual uplift I had received from attendance at Mass—although the latter is not to be discounted. All mythologies have roots running deep into the collective unconscious, all have power, perhaps all tap the ultimate Power which is beyond human comprehension.

Within a day or two after the momentous phone call from Harry Lawton, I received a letter from Anne Jennings, asking that I give her permission to seek my transfer to an institution in Hemet where she and her husband Bill could keep an eye on me. Deeply as I appreciated the offer, I urged her to hold back on making any inquiries, since I feared it might jeopardize my Public Health Service subsidy and might ultimately result in things becoming worse for me at Golden Mesa if the transfer proved impossible for me. My letter to Anne (October 17, 1974) expresses apprehension over "rocking any boats."

Then I received another telephone call which was destined to alter drastically the course of my life. After some difficulty, my beloved Micki Michelson succeeded in getting through to me. On this day of writing (December 2, 1976) Micki has found certain letters written after her call which allow me

155

to assign it an approximate date—probably the second week in October, since the earliest of these letters is dated October 16, 1974.

Ralph and Micki Michelson and their daughter, Ingrid, had been on an extensive journey in their motor home. They had visited relatives in New England and in Florida, and had returned to their home in Poway, California, in time for the beginning of the school year. During all this time they had not heard from me or about me. Knowing that some fifteen years prior to this time I had deeply desired to live on the desert, they assumed that I was happily situated with Georgia in the Chemehuevi Valley. But Micki, who, I firmly believe, has latent psychic powers, had become increasingly uneasy about me. When the Michelsons learned of my plight, they determined, after due consideration, to offer me a home with them. Micki had observed conditions in convalescent homes and knew that such an environment was not for me.

She obtained my address from Marjorie Misbeek, I believe—Micki and Marjorie, it will be remembered, were the two friends who had rescued me from a somewhat desperate dilemma in Los Angeles in March of that same year. A phone call would be better, quicker, and more definite than writing. Micki attempted to put one through. She was told the same thing that Harry had been told—I was in bed and could not be disturbed. But Micki also is a very forceful person. She said that she was calling long distance, would be calling back in exactly one hour, and they were to have me ready to receive the call.

She called at the time specified. I, of course, was not at the nurses' station waiting for the call; I was still "in bed and could not be disturbed." Then she turned up her forcefulness to full volume, and again I was hustled into a wheelchair and brought to the telephone.

This time I know I wept. It was like a dream, like one of those rare and beautiful dreams in which the long-dead loved one suddenly appears alive and well. To be offered a home, a refuge, was almost beyond comprehension. But abruptly

I realized that to accept this offer would involve a complication of which I had almost lost sight.

In my letter of the sixteenth—it must have been written the day after the phone call—I expressed my profound gratitude, then went on to say that I could contribute a small amount towards living expenses:

> More no doubt if . . . I get Social Security income—and more still if I live long enough to collect royalties and the books prove not to be duds. I really feel like saying "Take me in now." But it has meant a great deal to Georgia to plan to have me with her and I feel I should by all means give it another try if her health improves to the point where it is feasible. As she is now, it wouldn't do at all. . . . Still I hope it will work out eventually for me to come back to Poway with no hurts and no regrets on either side. The desert has its fascination—but oh, Micki, I don't want to die in it.

From this passage it is obvious that my old and quite irrational fear of dying in the desert was still active. Reason tells me that given the finality of death, nothing is less important than its locale; but in this particular matter I continue to be unreasonable. In the letter I wrote more of Georgia's prospects and of my own improved health (how ironical!—it was actually much worse than I realized), then I went on:

> I love the atmosphere of your home, I love Poway and feel so at home there. For a time I really feared that if things went wrong with Georgia (which God forbid!) I would have no alternative but to spend the rest of my life here. We are three beds to a room. There are more mentally deranged on this corridor than not and this "new wing" is supposed to be the best. Right now my roommate (the other one [Lura], the sane one [Florence] is going home Sunday) is trying to decide if this is her room, and an old lady [Alma] is singing "Silent Night." In a qua-

> very voice, another [Lillian] is calling out to every
> passerby "Come here, darlin', I love you," and
> a man [Hank] is swearing because he has to be
> shaved. That is just part of it.

It wasn't really necessary to go into such details with
Micki. She has seen what such places are like. She knew
that I did not belong there—no one *belongs* in that kind of an
environment, but the surplus old are one of America's terrible
problems. Sometimes, even when there are kind and loving
relatives—as in the case of Mrs. Chancellor and (temporarily)
Florence and Marie Haase—some sort of nursing facility seems
the only solution. Micki must have wondered that I hesitated
and temporized. My quandary about Georgia was very real.
There may also, however, have been another latent fear. What
if my physical condition worsened? I would have lost my status as a Reservation resident, there would be nothing left but
warehousing in some dreadful state institution. Besides, I now
felt that with a way of escape open, I could endure a little
longer with equanimity. I seem to remember that Micki wrote
back something about making the patio into another room,
which would take some time; and I responded that the delay
would be all right with me.

There were a few days—a very few—during which I felt that
I might now be reasonably content to stay in Golden Mesa almost indefinitely—even for six months or more if necessary.
There was the increasingly respectful treatment accorded me,
the talk of making a place for my typewriter. (Imagine trying
to type in a room with Lura and Mrs. Chancellor!) I persuaded
myself that I must wait and see how things turned out with
Georgia and only go to the Michelsons as a last resort. Some
now forgotten straw broke the camel's back of my optimism.
On the 22nd of October I wrote:

> Sunday was a bad day here and suddenly I
> thought, "Why should I stay in this place till
> Georgia gets well—which may take longer than we
> think—when Micki and Ralph are ready to take me

in? So I immediately wrote to Georgia . . . explaining that you had offered to come and get me, that
I would be much happier with you than in this
"place of (sometimes) torment."

So concerned was I still about seeming to disrupt a family
plan that I even asked Micki to check with Georgia by telephone, to see if it would be "all right" with her. I doubt if
this was ever accomplished, for I think by this time Georgia
was spending most of her time in a hospital in the Los
Angeles area.

With my departure now a definite prospect (though a part
of my mind still refused to accept it), I became bolder and
more outgoing. Although the Halloween Party held no appeal,
I did attend a morning coffee. It was an unfortunate experience. The coffee was fresh and hot, the cookies more edible
than anything we usually had for dessert. But it came about
that I sat at a table with a couple who had just arrived—had,
I believe, been brought to Golden Mesa that very morning.
Obviously they were a couple who had been married for the
better part of their lives, who had lived and loved and worked
and fought together, had prospered and raised a family, and
declined at last into ill health and perhaps—in the wife's
case—partial senility. From their conversation, I gathered
that they had been living with a daughter and that it hadn't
worked out.
  The old woman, wiping futilely at tears that wouldn't stop
flowing, kept demanding, "Vhere is mine Emma? Vhen vill
mine Emma come to take me home?"
  The old man, just as brokenhearted but with a clearer grasp
of circumstances, did his best to play his husbandly role of
comforter. "This is our home now. It's a pretty good place.
We gotta have people take care of us."
  He repeatedly urged his wife to drink coffee, to taste
a cookie. "Drink some coffee, Mama, you'll feel better. Here,
look! This is a good little cookie!"
  Impatiently she pushed away the hand that held the cook-

ie. "Shut up, Sharley! Shut up! I vant mine Emma!" And then at last, from the depths of despairing realization, "Mine Emma vill not come."

I returned to Room 36, terribly despondent. Then back to the dining room at noon, then back to the room again. After morning coffee and iced tea at noon, I felt the need to go to the bathroom. I don't remember how I got there—whether the borrowed walker had been left within reach or whether, for a change, someone had condescended to answer the call button which I now insisted be placed where I could reach it at all times. However it came about, I was seated on the commode when the Head Nurse arrived to interview me.

I had seen little of her until it was definitely known that I was preparing to leave Golden Mesa. The position in which she found me was not calculated to reinforce a sense of human dignity; but it clearly did not occur to my visitor that I could have talked to her more happily—and probably more reasonably—if she had first called someone to assist me back into my wheelchair. (In Golden Mesa, such menial tasks were beneath the professional dignity of nurses—except, rarely, of a young and newly arrived LVN.)

She began by stating, with a nice mingling of reproach and solicitude, "I hear you are not happy here. I hear you want to leave us."

I wasn't happy (who could be happy under such circumstances?) and I did want and hope to leave. Momentarily speechless, I didn't know whether to shake or nod my head. Somehow I managed to indicate that what she had heard was correct.

In a somewhat wounded tone, she demanded specifics. What, exactly, was making me unhappy?

Again I was at a loss. I didn't want to break out into accusations about the dreadful food, the mingling of the mentally incompetent with the mentally competent, and the dehumanizing effect of treating everyone as senile; the underpaid, frequently incompetent and occasionally callous aides and the absence of any sort of medical care except for a patient obviously in extremis. I felt cowed and timid, as Florence and I had felt when we slavishly assured the dietician that we were satisfied with our food. After all, I had to remain in Golden Mesa for a time, days or possibly even weeks. To be absolutely truthful, I still felt no inner conviction that I would ever leave. If I said too much, there could be reprisals.

When the Head Nurse urged me for detailed complaints, I came up with the matter of not being allowed to lie down in the daytime. "If I could only stretch out for fifteen minutes," I said, "it would make all the difference in the world."

Indignantly, she assured me that there was no such rule. "Who told you there was?" she demanded. "Who told you there was such a rule?"

I replied that none of the "girls" permitted the beds to be disturbed.

"They have no authority," she returned indignantly, "no authority at all. When you want to lie down and rest, you speak to a nurse about it. Someone with a cap"—she tapped her own starched and immaculate headgear—"the ones in caps are the only ones with authority."

They also were the ones we saw only briefly and with whom we seldom exchanged words. A nurse came in with morning and evening medication, sometimes briefly before noon for those who needed medication before meals, but more often this was administered hastily in the dining room. Once in a long while a "girl" took alarm at some symptom and sent for a nurse—that had happened when the aide whose too-enthusiastic scrubbing had rubbed the skin from my crotch had been alarmed at the sight of bleeding. But such occurrences were infrequent. As a rule, in Golden Mesa only doctors were harder to contact than nurses.

Faced with a suggestion of such patent absurdity that if I wanted to lie down all I had to do was contact a friendly nurse, my first impulse was to swear. I almost said, "How the hell do you think I'm going to get hold of a nurse every time my back aches?" Of course I made no such retort. I merely thanked her and said that in the future I would do as she suggested.

"Well," she asked briskly, "is there anything else troubling you?"

Suddenly my heart brimmed over. I began carefully enough: "I don't doubt that this is a superior institution. I don't doubt that it is run better than most such places. But I find the whole atmosphere distressing. Why, just this morning at the coffee hour, this poor old couple . . . " I had intended to describe the situation dispassionately. To my rage and humiliation, I found myself bursting into tears. Remember, I was at a disadvantage, seated in cramped quarters on a commode with an authority figure standing over me. "It was heartbreaking," I stammered between sobs, "absolutely heartbreaking. This poor old couple . . . "

"They've just arrived," the Head Nurse said soothingly. "Why, I think they only came this morning." (As if I didn't realize the poignancy of the newly arrived!) "Give them a little while to adjust," she continued. "In a week they'll be perfectly happy, perfectly at home!"

In my entire time at Golden Mesa I never saw a perfectly happy person except one who was about to leave or one who was self-deluded into thinking departure imminent. There was no use disputing this point with the Head Nurse. But I must have said something about my own lack of intelligent companionship, for she was quick to point out that I had my intellectual peers.

"There's Maurice," she said. "He was a performing musician; and Hilda was Head Nurse in a *big* hospital." They were happy here—why couldn't I be?

"What was Maurice's instrument?" I asked.

"The banjo, I believe." Then, becoming more positive, "He played the banjo beautifully."

I was being offered the mental placebo of the presence under the same roof of a former banjo player and a senile or brain-damaged former Head Nurse. If I had attempted to answer, I would have become hysterical. I simply maintained a stubborn silence.

"I see," she said finally, sounding more than a little offended. "You just don't feel this place is for you."

"No," I agreed wearily, glad that the interview was over, "I just don't feel it's for me."

Micki and I were keeping up a constant exchange of letters, but our letters were crossing. There was never a direct answer to whatever one of us had written. I tried desperately for several days to telephone, but all my efforts were smoothly frustrated. Obviously I wasn't, in my depleted condition, as forceful as either Harry or Micki. Or perhaps I was merely trying from the wrong end. Finally a letter arrived with a definite date—November 10th. I had to confirm this date at once, I could not bear not to make an immediate reply. Elaine Haase made the phone call for me from her home and assured me that there was no misunderstanding. Even then I did not really believe that I would ever leave.

In a futile but continuing effort to find an interest for their mother, Mrs. Chancellor's daughters had rented a television set for her. The indispensable Joe installed it in the corner where Florence's special chair had been—the nook which was to accommodate my typewriter if I became a permanent resident. Joe adjusted the set and left it running. Mrs. Chancellor promptly remarked, "I don't think anyone's listening to this thing," walked over and turned it off. Lura was disgusted; she would have liked it on all day. I would have enjoyed the news broadcasts, but preferred silence to a constant flood of inanities.

Since our daily ritual with the calendar had been established, Mrs. Chancellor had seemed somewhat less restless. But now the rumor of my imminent departure had filtered through her mental fog and was causing some uncertainty. She confided to her daughters that she really didn't care to remain while her "landlady" was away on a visit; she thought she herself might go somewhere until the landlady returned. This was almost more than I could endure—to think that another unfortunate had found Golden Mesa bearable because of the compassion I had felt towards her! Surely it was the sensed compassion more than the small outward courtesies that had given partial respite to a restless soul.

During the latter part of my stay in Golden Mesa, an aide

named Barbara had frequently been our morning "girl." Florence and I both liked her very much, and since Florence had left I had come to depend upon her more and more. Barbara did me many small kindnesses. She washed out my slips by hand and hung them in the bathroom to dry. Since I only had two, and the laundry was both rough on clothing and apt to misplace it, this service was much appreciated.

At Golden Mesa, the noncharity patients' laundry was either done at home by the patients' families (if any), or charged for at the rate of ten dollars per month. Lotion and powder were also provided for privately or charged to the patients' accounts. Just before Florence went home I learned that an additional charge was also made for chux—those disposable paper squares which were placed over the bottom sheet to take care of any "accident" resulting from incontinence or a carelessly placed bedpan. Since I had been told that I was classified as a private patient, I had expected to be presented a bill for these extras (with the exception of lotion and powder, which I purchased for myself with the assistance of Ann Keim or some friendly aide), but none ever arrived. I noticed that about the first of November I began to have a couple of soft diapers placed under me instead of a chux, which suited me very well because I found the chux uncomfortable. I wonder, in retrospect, if bills for certain small extras were not being submitted to the local Bureau of Indian Affairs office. Perhaps that would account in part for the increased pressure which Mr. King was attempting to apply through his gentle and embarrassed intermediary. During her last visit poor Rosita tried her best to insist that I sign an application and have my Social Security check sent directly to Golden Mesa. She reiterated, with attempted firmness, that that was what Mr. King wanted me to do. I dismissed the whole matter with the positive statement that I was about to leave; I would have my Social Security checks sent to my new address in California. This last interview left me more eager than ever to leave before the month was out. I did not think it possible to protect my tiny income for another thirty days.

And now, at last, after Elaine's report of her telephone call to Micki, the date was finally set. My one friend in Phoenix, whose address I had obtained from Micki, had heard, also from Micki, of my plight and attempted to call me, but again I was not summoned to the phone. She couldn't come in person, because she and her husband were about to leave town. But had I, in the preceding weeks, been allowed to ask information for her number (or had I had the wit to ask a visitor or social worker to help me), I might have had a friendly visitor of my own, a link to the world of sanity and reality.

I said good-bye to all the more friendly aides and to Deanna, the housekeeper to whom I felt so close. I wrote down addresses and promised to send cards. I gave away the redwood box my date-nut candies had come in; Callie asked for it, but didn't come to get it when she said she would, so it went to someone else. I hadn't really anything else to leave behind except my goodwill to those who had earned it.

On the night of November tenth the Dragon Lady came and talked to me. Incredible as it seems, I think I remember that she let down the railing and sat on the edge of my bed. We talked freely, one human being to another. We talked about her place in the mountains, among the tall pines that she loved, and we talked about my books. Relaxed in normal conversation, her mouth did not look at all saurian. Perhaps it was the constant tension of her work that had given her that forbidding expression. She began, suddenly, to speak of that work. She said that when she gave medication she frequently had "to look in their mouths to see if they'd swallowed it." "Oh, no, surely not!" I replied. "Oh, yes," she insisted. "You'd be surprised to what lengths some of them will go to keep from swallowing a capsule." She described just how she had to force the mouth open. So, politely but unmistakably, she let me know that she had only pretended to allow me to win our contest. At the end of our conversation, she gave me the Chloral Hydrate capsule, and I secreted it in my cheek as usual, and we said goodnight and good-bye. The game was played out to its last move. I am eternally grateful to her for not subjecting me to the ultimate humiliation of having my mouth pried open.

One of the evening aides was new on the job; new, ill-trained, good-hearted, and profoundly stupid. Standing by my bed, she asked on this last night, "Do you like rings?"

"What?" I asked. I had heard her without understanding her. I certainly wore no rings, no jewelry of any kind.

"Rings," she repeated, raising her voice as one does when speaking to the deaf. "See, rings!" She pulled a handful of unbelievably cheap rings—they looked like premiums from Cracker Jack or cereal boxes—out of her uniform pocket. "You can wear some if you want," she offered. "You can have some to keep."

"Thank you," I responded cruelly, "I have never cared for dime-store jewelry."

It wouldn't have hurt me to be more gracious. But this girl hadn't known how to do anything. She seemed at a loss when asked to do very simple things, and I was relieved when her companion did them instead.

By what seemed unbelievable good fortune, Barbara was my helper on the morning of November tenth. She had had superior training in a hospital somewhere in the cold country— Minnesota or Michigan, I can't at the moment remember which. She had been divorced and very recently remarried. Even though her two small boys were "back east" with their father, she fairly glowed with happiness. Happiness and fulfillment seem to act differently on different people. Some turn inward; some, like Barbara, must share their heart's treasure with everyone. I have wondered if I was merely a recipient of her overflowing joy or if she would have been just as kind if her personal life had been drab and hopeless.

Barbara packed my few belongings, helped me to sort out my own books from the ones that must be returned, gave me a shower, dressed me in the one good dress brought over from Chemehuevi Valley. There was nothing to wear under it but a slip; I had almost forgotten about bras and panty hose.

The day before I had arranged to purchase a used walker (not Maurice's) from Golden Mesa. I thought the price exorbitant, but my check was accepted without question.

Also on the preceding afternoon I had wheeled myself down to the office opposite the main nurses' station—the office jointly occupied by the Grasshopper Lady and the bookkeeper. I figured that I should have close to ninety-six dollars on deposit there, including the seventy-three I had received from Blue Cross. When, after the usual long delays, I was able to ask about my money, I was told there would be someone there the next day (even though it was a Sunday) to check it out for me. But there was a strange evasiveness about the amount. Apropos of nothing at all, the violet-eyed book-keeper remarked, "That Mr. King is a regular devil." I began to fear that a demand was about to be made for Social Security payments I had received while in the institution. Even the next day this nagging anxiety was still with me.

By nine-thirty or ten o'clock on the morning of the tenth I was ready to go. I made tentative plans. If the Michelsons came when it was nearly noon, perhaps I would invite them into the dining room with me. Golden Mesa usually furnished trays to people visiting patients (although I never noticed any of Mr. Naha's visitors eating with him!), and Sunday noon the food would not be too unspeakable. There would be roasted or fried chicken (compensating for the small cold waffle on a paper plate which we had had for breakfast). With these daydreamings I was actually trying to make myself believe that I was about to leave. I still could feel no inward conviction that this day would be any different from those that had preceded it. But at its end I would refuse to break mentally, like poor Lillian; and I would try my hardest not to let my tears stream like Mrs. Delacourt's.

The midday meal came and went. I sat in my wheelchair writing letters. Everything was packed, but the purse Mabel Axtell had given me was large enough to accommodate a small writing tablet. I was determined to conduct myself as usual, to keep nerves and emotions under tight control.

Something drew my eyes to the window. A tall pretty blond girl was standing there, holding in her arms a white cat on a leash. I did not have my glasses on, so her face was indistinct. I could not quite place her. My first thought was that an off-duty aide, remembering my love for animals, had brought her cat to show me.

Then a sound at the door made me look around and there stood Micki, with Ralph, quiet and kind as always, just back of her. Micki always signed her letters with a little round, smiling face, the way some children draw the sun. Now her real face, flushed and smiling and filled with love, with its strong crown of blond hair, was to me like the rising sun, like the beginning of a day that I had thought never to see, signaling my return from Limbo to the land of the living.

I think my first words were, "That's Ingrid outside with her cat!"

Micki has told me since that I was almost unrecognizable: small, frail, wrinkled, with the pasty-white coloring that accompanies extreme anemia.

Barbara was on hand to help us. I was wheeled down to the office. A nurse unlocked the cabinet where medicines were kept and gave me everything that bore my name. Mostly they were quite innocuous: eye drops, Benadryl, Vitamin C, Darvocet. There were also the Chloral Hydrate capsules and the full plastic container of aspirins, which fortunately no one had attempted to give me. Everything bore the name of Dr. Hawke, the doctor I had never seen and who had never seen me. Then I was handed a suspiciously slim envelope containing my cash.

We went out through the foyer, through the outside door into the sunlight. The Michelsons had brought their motor home, although I had written that it wouldn't be necessary on my account. After sitting all day long, day after day in a wheelchair, I could certainly sit up for a drive to Poway. Now I had a few last moments of panic—I didn't see how I was ever going to be hoisted up into the vehicle. That operation was rather quickly accomplished. It impressed me as precarious but not too difficult. Soon I was glad to lie down on the wide bed already made up at the rear of the motor home.

My bedmates were the white cat, Tuffy, whose build and blue eyes showed Siamese ancestry, although the pale yellow rings encircling his tale provided evidence of a more plebian forebear; and Barney, the obese, intelligent black and white dog. Barney is with us still, but Tuffy has since departed the Michelson household (and presumably this vale of tears) under somewhat mysterious circumstances.

Lying beside the friendly animals as more and more desert miles stretched between us and Phoenix, I found at length the courage to open my purse, take out the envelope, and count my cash. I had been given precisely twenty-three dollars. The seventy-three dollars from Blue Cross, reimbursing me for medical expenses, incurred long before I ever heard of Golden Mesa, had been appropriated by that institution. I was disappointed, for I had intended to hand the money to Ralph or Micki to apply to household expenses. No matter! It seemed a small price to pay for freedom.

Looking back now at my last two encounters with the office personnel, I am amused at our mutual uneasiness. I was fearful that I would not be released until I had met some impossible financial demand; they were afraid I would demand an accounting for moneys deposited. It is quite possible that I owed the Home at least seventy-three dollars for unspecified extras. If so, an itemized bill should have been presented and a receipt given. The underhanded way in which the transaction was conducted seems to me to label it as petty theft. But again, no matter! Far worse things might have befallen me.

Crossing the state line at Yuma was cause for jubilation. Somewhere along the road we bought food. I remember an oven-fresh, sugary doughnut that tasted better than anything I had eaten for months.

The sunset glow deepened and faded. We watched the starry vault of heaven and talked about flying saucers.

Shortly before midnight we pulled into the driveway of

the home that, with the exception of a ten months' interlude with my daughter Margaret and several hospitalizations, has been my home ever since. The prison or refuge (however you care to view it) called Golden Mesa Nursing and Convalescent Home is forever behind me. The iron door that had clanged shut upon my heart opened gently and set me free.

Proving, if one cares to consider it in that light, that miracles are possible.

EPILOGUE —
Before and After *Limbo*

In November, 1974, when the Michelson family rescued Carobeth Laird from Limbo in Phoenix, she was entering an eighth life. Her prospects were enticing but precarious. Although her books, *Encounter with an Angry God* and *The Chemehuevis*, had been accepted for publication, and *Encounter* was already in type, the dismal question was: Would she live to see even one of them make a public appearance? She had been writing for a lifetime, never doubting her vocation. Friends at Malki Museum Press, her publisher, believed that both works were masterpieces. And she had more books in her!

For details on Carobeth Laird's early years, the reader is referred to *Encounter* and the Foreward to *The Chemehuevis*. Briefly sketched, these are her "seven lives" prior to November, 1974.

• She was born in 1895 and spent a lonely and fantasy-ridden girlhood in Coleman, Texas, the overprotected only child of squabbling parents who had been married twenty years before her birth.

• She moved to San Diego with her parents in 1913, pregnant following an ill-fated love affair. She entered young womanhood with a baby, little in the way of formal education, a frenetic imagination, and a fanatic thirst for knowledge.

171

- She married her summer-school professor, the maverick (and legendary) linguist and ethnographer John Peabody Harrington, in 1916, bore him a child, and spent several bizarre, deprived but fascinating years as his field assistant and general factotum.

- In 1919, when she was twenty-four, she met a Chemehuevi tribesman, George Laird, exactly twice her age, who became first her language informant and then her lover, while she and he recorded Chemehuevi lore for the Smithsonian Institution under Harrington's direction.

- She left Harrington in 1920, obtained a divorce from him in 1923, and married George Laird the same year. They lived in Poway, California (near San Diego), eking out a living, raising their family of five children, and continuing to record data on Chemehuevi language, customs, and belief.

- After George Laird's death in 1940, she was destitute, both financially and emotionally. She rallied to support herself and her family, making her living as a practitioner in the Christian Science Church. Over the years, she assumed a role as a vital force within the church.

- In 1960, she resigned her membership in the Christian Science Church and entered into a period of obscurity, declining health, crippling arthritis, and dependency on her children. But also, and more importantly, during this time there was a great intellectual "explosion," involving voracious reading and considerable writing, including poetry and fiction as well as the manuscripts for *The Chemehuevis* and *Encounter with an Angry God*.

Throughout each of these seven lives, Carobeth Laird was teaching herself the art of writing. In the eighth life which she faced in November, 1974, she had the prospect that her art would finally reach an audience. But, could she hold out?

That November, as she left Arizona, Carobeth Laird was fully recovered from the emergency surgery described so dramatically in *Limbo*, but she was in frightful pain from a deteriorated hip and she suffered from a collection of symptoms and disorders which would be depressing to detail here.

Ill as she was, suffering as she was, Mrs. Laird decided that she must write *Limbo*. The title was with her from the moment she decided to write it. Her Malki friends—of whom Harry Lawton (Chairman of Malki's Editorial Board) and I were the most insistent—promoted the project, certain that she could write about the simple horrors of life as a nursing-home patient better than anyone else. She thought she might do others a service by writing from her own experience, ghastly as it would be to recollect.

Malki could not offer to publish *Limbo*, since the subject would not fall within the guidelines of this small, nonprofit, and volunteer Indian museum's anthropological press, but Malki editorial workers promised to help her find a publisher.

Late in 1974, or early 1975 . . . she is not certain which . . . Mrs. Laird made a start on *Limbo*. Her condition soon declined so seriously that she was unable to continue writing, and in April, 1975, she was hospitalized in Escondido, California, for major surgery . . . hip implantation. Once again, she made a dramatic recovery and her new hip gave her the first relief she had had from the constant pain of many years. Still she was not well, but her doctors in Escondido did not offer any solid information or solutions.

Mrs. Laird was now living with a daughter, Margaret, in Del Mar, California, where she stayed for about a year. In Del Mar, Mrs. Laird received assistance from an able physical therapist, Sheila Smith, and she made steady progress with her boring and difficult program of therapy. One fine day, she graduated from the orthopedic walker which—apart from a wheelchair—had been her only means of locomotion for years to a set of four-pronged metal canes, the "sticks" she still uses.

Her preliminary work on *Limbo*, about fifty pages of it, had been lost in the shuffle between Poway and Del Mar, so Mrs. Laird started over again after her surgery. The working conditions were difficult, but she was with members of her family, which was a source of contentment for her.

Harper's Bookletter published in May, 1975, two months prior to the publication of *Encounter with an Angry God*, a long and enthusiastic review of the book by journalist Tom Wolfe. Wolfe had learned about Mrs. Laird and her work while she was still in Arizona Limbo. His generous efforts on her behalf with New York magazine publishers was without a doubt the critical factor in finding a general audience for *Encounter*. The odds against the success of a first book by an aged unknown author from an obscure publisher without a budget for promotion were enormous.

When *Encounter* was published in July, 1975—coincidentally with Mrs. Laird's eightieth birthday—this memoir of her two marriages drew rave reviews in major publications throughout the country, and Mrs. Laird herself came in for a flurry of attention from newspapers, magazines, radio and telelvision stations. She loved it. Through all the interviews, speaking engagements, autograph parties, telephone calls, correspondence, and drop-in visitors, she plugged away at *Limbo*. But she was not well.

Paperback rights to *Encounter* were negotiated by Mrs. Laird's agent Gordon Molson in November, 1975, at the BooksWest Book Fair in Los Angeles, where she was a featured speaker and where she had a standing-room-only audience for her address.

Early in 1976, Mrs. Laird moved back to the Michelson home in Poway. At times, she required full-time care, which Maj (Micki) Michelson, a trained nurse, came forward to provide. In April, 1976, on the edge of collapse, Mrs. Laird undertook a trip to an anthropological convention in San Francisco, where she delivered a scholarly paper. Upon her return to Poway, she was again hospitalized, this time at Sharp Memorial Hospital in San Diego. Her physicians—Dr. Robert K. Bench and Dr. Joel Barrish—pulled her through one more seige of major surgery.

Mrs. Laird had two hiatal hernias, one of them enormous. A great wad of intestine had poked up into her chest cavity where it had collapsed one lung and partially collapsed the second. The heart itself was being pushed out of position. The surgery involved reconstruction of her diaphragm and the rearrangement of her vital organs back into their normal positions. Obviously it had been a dying woman who had been delivering papers and writing her book, granting interviews and captivating TV audiences. Before he operated, Dr. Bench told me he could not understand how she had managed to survive without the operation.

They allowed me to enter Sharp's intensive care unit shortly after Mrs. Laird was wheeled out of surgery. As she lay, plugged into tubes and needles, her dark eyes were wide open and snapping, and she spoke emphatically. The plastic breathing apparatus over her mouth made it very difficult to understand her, so I leaned close. Clearly, she was not conscious. She was not talking to me, nor does she remember the moment. She was chanting in a rhythmic, timed cadence—the cadence of a heartbeat: "Live . . . Live . . . Breathe . . . Breathe . . . Live . . . Live . . . " That valiant life force, the power she has demonstrated over and over again to will the body's recovery, was working for her again.

In July, 1976, after an initial recovery from the complex surgery, Mrs. Laird again collapsed and was readmitted to Sharp for treatment of congestive heart failure. This time, her doctors thought surely she was gone. ("This is an *old* lady . . . her parts are wearing out," said one.) But she was not yet ready to give up and, once again, she confounded science by refusing to die. She still had so much work to do; she still hadn't seen her second book published.

In September of 1976, after unbelievable delays, *The Chemehuevis* finally appeared in print—more than five years after Malki Museum Press had contracted for its publication. This vast, exquisitely written book on George Laird's tribe and language also received stupendous reviews. Once again, Mrs. Laird became a media event. Once again, she was an honored guest at the BooksWest Book Fair . . . and still . . . she typed away at *Limbo*.

She finished this book in December, 1976. I did the initial editing, and I must say I didn't have very much to do. Mrs. Laird found a New York agent, Helen Brann, who was enthusiastic about the book's prospects and who worked determinedly for its publication. But Helen could not track down a major Eastern publisher willing to take on the risk and burden of *Limbo*.

Every house had a different reason for rejecting the manuscript: "Too detached." "Not detached enough." "Maybe I'm a monster, but it doesn't move me." "I seriously doubt that Carobeth Laird wrote this book." "Needs more plot." "I love Carobeth and admire her writing, but I can't sell her book." In the spring of 1978, the manuscript for *Limbo* was returned to Mrs. Laird.

Happily, Jonathan Sharp of Chandler & Sharp Publishers, a friend of Malki Museum Press and of Carobeth Laird, had offered the year before to consider publishing her book if she couldn't find a mainline commercial publisher. And, so it is that *Limbo* is finally emerging in print.

Between the time *Limbo* was completed (December, 1976) and this date (January, 1979) Carobeth Laird has regularly contributed scientific papers to *The Journal of California Anthropology*. She has periodically given talks in the San Diego, Riverside County, and Los Angeles areas. She was honored by Ballantine Books at the American Booksellers Association convention in San Francisco.

In May, 1978, she flew to New York as the guest of grade-school children in Malvern, Long Island, who had become interested in her books and who had become pen pals of hers. The children raised the money to bring Mrs. Laird and her daughter Rosaleen back East to visit with them. That visit became the subject of a *Parade* magazine cover story (July 30, 1978), which brought a flood of fan mail to Poway (and, ironically, a number of publishing offers from the East).

But the trip exhausted her, and in the summer of 1978 she collapsed again and was readmitted to Sharp Memorial Hospital. Again, she pulled off one of her patented comebacks. Although she is still not as strong as she was a year ago, she continues to gain strength and she is in better health than when I first met her in 1971, when she was (only) seventy-six.

Today, she is well into a second volume of Chemehuevi lore: *Mirror and Pattern: George Laird's World of Chemehuevi Mythology*. As she set to this work, she also embarked on an intensive study of comparative mythology. She was eighty-two then. Now, she is also dictating material which will be included in another book of memoirs: *Pilgrim and Stranger*. In July, 1979, she will be eighty-four years old.

For nearly thirty years, Carobeth Laird was a member of the Christian Science Church, and as noted above, after the death of her husband, George, she made a living as a Christian Science practitioner. During this era, she also published articles in the church journal on metaphysics. She was a famous practitioner, with many amazing (and official) healings credited to her. Even her written word has healed, as her correspondence attests. Her Christian Science discipline—without the intellectual strictures of the church—still serves her well today. She says she would have been dead long ago without it. She has been her own best physician for many years, assisted by skilled and concerned members of the medical profession.

But even the greatest physicians often need help. In the Michelson family, to whom this book is dedicated, and particularly in Micki Michelson, Carobeth Laird found the help she needed to stay alive.

Those of us who love Mrs. Laird, those of us who honor her as an important writer and as a major scholar, those of the reading public whose lives have been enriched by her work, owe much to Maj Michelson's contribution to the continued presence and productivity of this remarkable woman.

Between 1974 and 1979, between the ages of seventy-eight and eighty-three, Carobeth Laird lived in a baffling succession of domiciles. She faced repeated hospitalizations in unfamiliar surroundings. She was all but dead six times, by conservative count. During this period, she was reduced to indigence but managed to scrape by. During this period, she had three books published and did considerable work on two others. She became a minor literary celebrity. She survived a succession of

family tragedies which transcend soap opera and which would
have broken the heart and spirit of one with less tenacity and
determination to survive.

We who are close to her have witnessed with awe the gothic
excesses of her astounding life and wonder what lies in the
future for Carobeth Laird. What will the ninth life be? Nothing at all could surprise us.

Anne Buffington-Jennings
Hemet, California
January, 1979